Mad Random

Claiming Life Out Of Chaos

SHIRES ✺ PRESS

4869 Main Street
P.O. Box 2200
Manchester Center, VT 05255
www.northshire.com

Mad Random: Claiming Life Out Of Chaos

©2014 Donna Miller

Cover Design by Patrick DiMascio

ISBN Number: 978-1-60571-225-3

Printed in the United States of America

America

Remember Joy!

Mad Random

Claiming Life Out Of Chaos

Donna Miller

My son painted the original artwork featured on the cover when
he was a fifteen-year high school student. He entitled it,
"Self Portrait of Freud." When asked what he was trying to express,
he answered, *"Just like Freud, you have to figure it out for yourself."*
This painting hangs over my desk and is a daily reminder to embrace
the chaos of our mad random world.

—Donna Miller

To Sam
for the miracles of joy, constancy and grace

For Christopher
Who always has my back

Acknowledgments

I am grateful to the amazing women in my life who show up
and do the work of living each day with joy and purpose.
The mental health and education professionals
who read and reread this book provided useful advice and
perspective that shines through.

Thank you to my editors
Anne Lesser of Anne Lesser Communications and
Victoria Wright of Book Mark Services for their
good sense and counsel.
I am also indebted Sandy Gelles-Cole.
Finally, thank you to the parents who have shared with me their
stories about children that challenged their best efforts to live in
harmony. I am in awe of you, and I wish you peace.

CHAPTER ONE

HOSTAGES

Jumpy and uncomfortable at my desk, I consider a third tea run in under an hour. An empty page glows on the computer screen, mocking my resolve to finish my self-imposed word count and shut down the machine. Most days, I try to exit the office before convincing myself that I'm not a writer. If I don't make it out in time, I'm likely to hit the want-ad pages, searching for retail sales positions and the promised discount on professional clothing I don't wear to sit alone in a room to write. The rest of the afternoon's productivity relies on more caffeine, pitiful pleading with an absent muse, and head-smacking the screen. Now I am moving my fingers over the keys in random patterns that fill up empty space with nonsense. I am done.

Rushing to the car, I can't move fast enough to distance myself from any part of this day's work that has survived the delete button. The trip to the grocery store is average, although I do buy ten cans of soup for ten dollars, knowing no one at home eats canned soup.

At home, my seventeen-year-old son, Jack, is pacing, hovering close to the front hallway as though he has been waiting for my arrival. At nearly six feet four inches tall, his presence in the tiny foyer throws a shadow across my five-foot frame. He is too close, too cheerful, and the hair on my arms tickles, a private antenna that senses his urgency.

"How was your day?" he asks with unexpected cheerfulness.

"Fine," I say, struggling with the groceries and tripping over his cat's outstretched body. Half the soup cans roll under the dining-room table.

"Could you help me here?" I crawl under the table to retrieve the unnecessary cream of mushroom soup, catching a glimpse of a recipe for green beans with fried onions. My family doesn't eat that either.

"Uh, I'm going to get some fresh air." Moving quickly through the kitchen, Jack stops at the back cabinet junk drawer to retrieve his set of car keys. His car keys are still my hostages, taken in response to his third speeding ticket in as many months. He owes us hundreds of dollars for the speeding fines. There are also attorney's fees for the negotiated plea bargain to avoid a suspended driver's license. I wonder again why we provided this incentive for him to view the whole experience as "no big deal" and then remember the promised insurance hike that would bring his premium cost up to mortgage payment.

"Not with my car, you aren't," I say automatically. After six weeks of suspended driving privileges, Jack knows he isn't taking the car. He can fix this. He has to pay the fines and go back to school.

"You're a fucking idiot," he says, tension rising in his voice.

Usually this level of vulgarity follows something more onerous than repetition of a rule he dislikes. A line of electricity travels down my left arm. Am I having a heart attack? No, it's

2

cataclysmic rage ignited by the horror of tonight and all the times he's been abusive and rude.

I think I actually hate him.

Jack is making it impossible to love him, so where am I? I cannot feel neutral about my own son. I do hate him. I drop the soup cans, and they roll under the table, hitting the cat. She spits at me, clawing at the air.

"Give me the keys."

Starting toward him, I reach for his hand. One sweep of his long arm and the keys are far above my head. Jangling them out of my reach, he seems to expect me to do a trick for a treat. Reason returns in time for me to back off. Boundaries he is well aware of will prevent a physical battle. He is too big, and I am too frightened of being hurt.

"Get out of my way, or I will hurt you." He seems to read my thoughts. Suddenly his father is at the doorway, taking in the sights and sounds greeting his arrival.

"What's going on?" Sam is quiet, expectant.

"Mom is an idiot. I'm leaving." Jack speaks to his dad with more restraint, always. It irritates me. Tonight I give in to a childish eruption.

"That's 'fucking idiot' to you."

Sam ignores my outburst.

"Not with the car, you aren't. You can't take the car." Sam is clear, speaking with the control I cannot marshal.

Moving with speed reserved for high-priority escapes Jack is out the door and into the waiting car. Sam repeats his warning. "Don't do it, Jack."

Already behind the wheel of my car, he adjusts the mirrors and seat to accommodate his long body. Sam and I watch as he races out of the driveway, leaving thin rubber traces at the top of the long hill.

Jack often threatens to take the car without permission. We have devised a plan for this behavior. We will immediately call the police to report a stolen vehicle. Jack knows this will be the consequence for his unauthorized use of my car, and so far the threat has worked.

Now he is gone, and neither one of us moves to make the call. Instead, Sam repeatedly calls Jack's cell phone to offer him the opportunity to return. The cell is off, and Sam's calls go straight to voice mail.

"Let's look for him before we call the police," Sam suggests.

For just a moment I imagine Jack in jail, safe and gone. It is not a bad visual. Disconcerted by my thoughts, I push them aside, trying to concentrate on the current crisis.

An hour later, we are still trying to find our son. I believe that he has lost control of the car, crashed into a guardrail, and tumbled dead in a ditch. My cell phone rings, and Jack's number flashes across the screen.

"Where are you?"

"I'm someplace you'll never find me. I hid the car. Leave me alone." The connection is gone.

I recap the news for Sam, and we turn the car toward home, calling the police before we are inside the door.

Our small-town police department sends an officer from the domestic violence unit. He arrives quietly, without flashing lights or sirens. The need to conceal my humiliation is almost as imperative as finding my son, so I am grateful for the secrecy. The officer explains that because Jack is a minor, and his parents are making the complaint, the policy is to handle the theft as a domestic dispute. Even minors picked up on a felony warrant spend at least the night in jail, maybe more.

"Let's try plan B first," he says. "I'll call his cell phone from your home phone. He won't suspect anything is up." Dialing the number we give him, Jack's angry "What?" carries across the room when he answers the phone.

"Jack, I'm a detective with the police. I'm with your parents. If you're not home in fifteen minutes, I will find you. When I do, you'll be hauled out of the car and cuffed. You'd better plan on some jail time." Jack is back in twelve minutes, incensed and defiant.

The officer confiscates his license and keys, telling Jack, "You won't need these. I want to talk to your parents. Leave us alone."

Watching my son climb the stairs to his bedroom, I think about getting a badge and a gun for myself.

The police officer is in his early thirties, a little more than half my age. I want to explain why we can't settle this family disciplinary issue without calling the police. It doesn't matter what this young officer thinks, but I am defensive about our worry and rage, anxious to let him know how hard we have tried to parent this child. The fatigue from the events of the last few hours settles around me. I just want to go to bed.

The officer is asking questions. "Does your son take any medications? How about a counselor? Is he seeing anyone?"

Sam supplies a shorthand version of the past seventeen years. "Jack is largely drug resistant, although we've been through numerous drug trials. Nobody knows exactly what is wrong with him. He's pretty bright, but that hasn't seemed to help."

Nodding at each detail, the officer makes notes on a long clipboard. I notice his handwriting, small and precise, and remember that Jack hasn't mastered cursive writing other than to sign his name. He prints slowly and reluctantly.

"Nobody has ever been able to help him very much," Sam repeats, looking to me for confirmation.

I can't explain the cycle of violence, remorse, and depression that defines Jack's life and menaces ours with constant unpredictability.

Sam and I stand up, and the officer takes his cue to wind up the interview. He gives us a copy of the police report, explaining that we need to follow up with the domestic violence counselors.

The officer explains that because of our son's emotional issues, we can ask the police to check on his welfare instead of reporting a felony, which carries automatic jail time and may result in a criminal record. "This way, you aren't faced with the decision about filing charges unless he commits a serious crime."

The officer is handing us a way out of other evenings that may be tangled up in the same blend of anger and fear. I want to assure him it will never happen again; that we won't need this service. My hands are moving, making little circles, but I can't put together a sentence. Odds are, we will call again. I am not even convinced we will make it through this night.

Before leaving, he stops in the doorway and turns to look at me, pulling his card out of his wallet. His name is John. "You seem like nice people. We see too many of these boys. I know he has problems, but I sure hope it works out. He's pretty young. Sometimes things do get better. If I can help, call me or someone else at this number." He places the card on the hall table. Standing at the open front doorway, John looks into my eyes and hesitates before he adds, "Don't ever let him hurt you."

"I'm careful. I'll be okay." I am talking to myself, but he must hear something that satisfies him, because he says good-bye, closing the door behind him.

Jack immediately materializes at the top of the stairs. "If you hadn't been here, I would have punched his face."

"You would also be in jail," his dad promises.

"Don't you get it? I don't care what happens to me. I don't fucking care." The bedroom door slams shut, echoing in the upstairs hallway. There is nothing left to fill the space but the look on Sam's face. Lines recede into his cheeks, tightening up his eyes. I can hear the words he doesn't speak. "I don't want to do this anymore," is right behind his eyes. Before I have a chance to offer something that is probably not useful, he covers his eyes with his hands and closes the topic for tonight. I catch the gleam of white cuffs at the bottom of his wrists and realize he hasn't changed clothes since coming home from work and that no one has had any dinner.

Near bedtime, Jack begins the bully dance. Shattering the brief serenity of the officer's presence in our home, he follows me around the house, outraged about a shirt I didn't wash. He threatens Sam with destroying an MP3 player because he has misplaced a video game he is convinced his father threw away. I have all the steps memorized. I can't look at my son. I am afraid of what I'll see in that face I once stared at for hours, loving each nuance as he changed and grew.

Memories chase around my mind. I reach for any assurance that might silence my resentment for this evening's drama. A murky mental picture is identified from a forgotten feel-good file, and I grab hold. It is afternoon fifteen years ago. Jack climbs into my lap and puts both arms around my neck, seeking a hug. His beautiful toddler face is there. I can smell the shampoo in his freshly washed hair. We count toes together, each time coming up with different number. "No," I say, "That's not right. Let's do it again." Laughing, we would start all over again and again.

The picture is lost as suddenly as it appeared; I can't hold on to the lines of his jaw, the clear blue eyes, and the smile that ignited my love affair with my son.

How did this family make our way to this destructive night, this night where love and memories die in the toxic haze of violence and insecurity?

Sam heads up the stairs to bed, telling me to wake him if I need him. Another recollection provides a welcome respite. It is years ago, and Sam is laughing at me as I climb up on a pool table in our local college-town bar. Pool cue behind my back, I make a totally illegal shot with both eyes closed. The eight ball drops right into the pocket, no bounce. Nice.

By midnight I still hadn't settled down. Afraid I'll hurt Jack if he comes too close, I try to keep my hands behind my back. From my elbows to the tips of my fingers, everything tingles with a sharp need to slap his face. Fear that I could commit violence against my child frightens me more than anything else.

"I won't hit him. I'm the adult." Silently repeating this mantra, I fight to set aside this necessity to strike out. It's no good; there isn't enough room in the house to contain my discomfort. I need to be outside. Grabbing the car keys, I run to our bedroom door to tell Sam I'm taking a drive. Sam isn't sleeping.

"It's really late. Can't you come to bed?" My husband worries about my growing habit of late-night drives. "Take your cell phone and don't go far," Sam warns me before he goes back to not sleeping.

Jack tries to block my progress out the door with his bigger body. I make a wide circle around him and slip through under his arm. In the car with the door locked, I hear him scream into the nighttime air: "Go ahead, run away. Fuck you!"

What might life have been like had I carried to term those three souls Sam and I conceived in love and hope? Each time, we listened as heartbeats started and mourned as the sounds of life quieted, eventually lost to us. My heart has never forgotten, but the pain lost its edge the day Jack came into our lives.

Unable to reach the child I love, I can't turn away from the anguish of his disabilities and the abuse that defines his relationship with Sam and me. Our lost babies left us before we knew the promise of their love. Loving Jack demands that we move through the chaos without any promise of success and learn to live with the fear for ourselves and for our son. Some nights we are done pretending that our family can sustain these constant assaults on our needs and our dreams. Jack's emotional intransigence has produced too many evenings spent in a dance of defiance, linking our awkward threesome in that exhausted waltz known to prizefighters who grip each other for balance until they are sent to their separate corners. No win. No loss. An unsatisfying draw that surely makes the punishment of the fight irrelevant.

CHAPTER TWO

LOST BOYS

Once on the road, I had no idea where to go. Fueled by too much coffee, I drove north on the highway until I saw the timeless shadow of the Adirondack Mountains sloping away from the sky in the hoary light of the deepening night. Anxiety began to compete with the coffee high, and I wondered if I could mix caffeine with Xanax. I needed a rest stop in order to make my pharmaceutical experiment. The dashboard clock blinked 2:00 A.M. Wearing a red down coat over a green nightshirt covered with glow-in-the-dark sheep that declare, "I am falling a-sheep," I hoped to keep public appearances to a minimum.

Stopping at a wide spot on the side of the highway, I opened the driver's visor. The lighted vanity mirror reflected unruly curls that only a lawn mower could tame. A black ski hat lying on the floor seemed like good cover, so I pulled it over my head. Now I looked like a robbery suspect caught on grainy film as I fled the bank. I started to laugh. It wasn't a happy laugh, but any sound is hopeful in the dark night at the side of the road.

At the service area I pulled into a nearly empty parking lot. Pushing through the swinging doors to the rest stop, I can say that the ski hat would have been far too dressy. Truck drivers, nearly sober teenagers, and a depressed cleaning crew seemed lost in the cavernous space. A halogen glare poured down from industrial lights, bouncing off the walls and back to the ceiling. Toilet-flushing sounds traveled from behind the food court to the front door. There was no line at the beverage counter. Still, it took five minutes for the server to finish her phone call to her mother so she could get my tea. Finally, she began to pull together the necessary cup and tea bag, filling my order without the slightest bit of grace.

"Two dollars and forty cents," is all she said. I was grateful for the lukewarm water and no-name tea. The Xanax slipped down my throat.

Back on the access road, I swung the car into the southbound lane. Searching the rearview mirror for a safe entry point onto the interstate, I felt my steering wheel pull to the right while the car tagged along, accelerating for an inevitable crash into the guardrail. The three people following me were not concerned with my imminent danger, loping along in an eerie dance. Walloping the brake pedal with my foot, the car came to a jerky stop just short of the road's shoulder. I turned around to substantiate the presence of the pedestrians I had seen in my rearview mirror. They were still there, closer now to the car's bumper.

Light filtered through one figure who seemed older and slower than the other two. Tugging at each other, their progress was erratic, walking together and then floating around each other. Their long coats gave off a paranormal luminosity. Underneath, each figure was clothed in layers of pants, dresses, and long scarves. Were they men or women? I couldn't tell. Reaching for the door, maybe to lock it, maybe to flee from the car, I was drawn back to my vigil in the mirror. White light materialized from the center of the grouping, flashing once before the three creatures broke form and rose up from the highway in long wisps of gray and yellow smoke.

Nothing was there.

I was terrified, trembling so badly that I jumped towards the passenger seat when someone pounded on the driver's side door. Peering at me through the glass, a lone man was waiting, looking worried. Tangled up in my seat belt, I crawled under the shoulder harness, freeing myself to open the driver's door.

"Are you all right? You just about hit that railing. Didn't you hear me honking?"

My expression and the glowing nightgown under my coat was enough to send him a few steps backward.

"What happened to those people?" I pulled at his hand. "What people? There weren't any people. Anybody on this road would get killed." His hand escaped my grasp, and he used it to lean against the door, listening to me ramble on about wobbly-legged car followers.

"Yes, there were. There were three people walking right behind my car. You must have seen them." I pleaded with him to share my vision.

"No, lady, there really wasn't anybody. You want me to call someone? Maybe you're too tired to drive?"

I took in a bellyful of air and let it out in the prescribed yoga fashion, willing a calmer voice so I could dismiss my roadside rescue service.

"I'm okay. Thanks, though. I'm fine." I couldn't hide my urgency to be alone.

What could have produced this ethereal father, son, and Holy Ghost who visited me on this never-ending night?

Eventually, he let go of my door, closed it, and tapped the hood as a cop might do after he's written a speeding ticket. This time I made it safely to the interstate, avoiding the rearview mirror completely.

Ten minutes later, my breathing finally calmed. The cell phone ring startled me. Grabbing it quickly, I saw Jack's number on the screen and opened the phone.

"Dad says you need to come home." He sounded slightly annoyed. Checking the light across the mountaintop, I saw that it was almost dawn, an unlikely time for Sam to say anything.

"I'm here. I'm coming back." Three or four more seconds passed in silence.

"Oh. I thought you might have gotten hurt."

"What made you think that?" I was actually interested. I wanted to talk to someone, even to Jack.

"Nothing. I just wondered where you went."

"I'll be home in an hour. Go to bed."

"Yeah, when I feel like it." The connection was cut, and I flipped the top closed, dropping the phone into the cup holder.

We were clear that I was not hurt.

The next exit was mine. I slowed down for the off-ramp, setting my inner automatic pilot that knows each turn in the road home. Memories of the 1997 book party ushering in the new Harry Potter adventure, *Chamber of Secrets*, pushed into my thoughts. Jack and I waited with hundreds of other wizards and warlocks until the midnight release of the book he would never read. Now I wished for one of Harry Potter's invisibility capes. I would disassociate my body from the mother/spouse that sat in the car. Sending her alone into the house, I would save my spirit by returning to a changed universe, seeking the comfort of anyplace that wasn't home.

13

Sam had left on the outside lights. Our bedroom night-light radiated through the upstairs window. Jack's windows were dark.

I flipped on the overhead light in the car, and these words in the police report caught my eye: If you have concerns about physical or emotional abuse, you should remove yourself and minor children from the premises as quickly as you can. Trained counselors can help you take these steps safely.

I left home two months after my seventeenth birthday, younger than my son is tonight. I was missed and welcomed back for the times when I needed to be home. I wondered if we would miss Jack or if we'd ever have the chance to find out.

It was a long walk through the front door.

CHAPTER THREE

WHAT LOVE ABIDES

Emotional disability sweeps up and carries children with normal intelligence whose behavior is edgy and provocative, often resulting in violent outbursts of profane language and physicality. Disruptive behavior, communication deficits, and erratic social development are all tied together with the cord of emotional disability. Schools first designed this catchall category, and it could open the door to services for children in obvious of help who carried little or no medical or mental health evidence to support a diagnosis or a treatment plan.

Few congenital disabilities can be isolated with a blood test or an evaluations protocol. Families who suspect that their child's development is abnormal often struggle through years of developmental and educational testing before a workable diagnosis emerges. If a child presents serious developmental or social delays during his first three years of life, he will soon be evaluated for a spot on the long road of pervasive developmental disorders (PDD).

Because of its baffling frequency during the last several decades, an especially bright light has been sited on attention deficit hyperactivity disorder (ADHD), conditions that describe children who can't or won't sit still, focus, or relate appropriately to their peers or adults.

ADD and ADHD claim a growing number of American school-aged children within its scope of dysfunction; as many as 3 to 5 percent by some estimates. Schools, communities, and pharmaceutical companies all have a stake in endorsing this unyielding focus on a child's ability to adapt to a world that demands structure and supervised activity. Many parents, me among them, remain unconvinced that the ADD/ADHD blitz and its attendant drug treatments and behavioral plans have brought relief to our troubled children, but enough progress has been made enough of the time to keep this diagnosis current. The explosion of medications, books, and teacher and parent training programs that began in the 1990s continues to swell the market today.

Stimulant medications, often the drug therapy of choice in treating the broad spectrum of symptoms that signify ADD/ADHD, are mostly benign and inexpensive to produce. In truth, almost everyone focuses better for a short time if they are given a stimulant. The debate will continue over treating this group of symptoms that is not really an illness. None of it was useful to our son.

Current world safety concerns, changing community structure, and the necessary obligations of working parents have meant that many young children have little time for free play. Young people are required to attend for longer periods of time than they were thirty years ago. This is not to say that a return to the lifestyle and values of 1950s middle-class America would ease life for a generation of struggling children. There have always been children who could not abide long days of structured activities and the accompanying expectation of more sophisticated learning and social skills. My son couldn't make it through a thirty-minute swim class when he was six years old. Other children thrive, moving from activity to activity, happily enriched by the dazzling array of choices available today.

When faced with a series of possible reasons for Jack's differences we sometimes picked up on a diagnosis and ran with it, seeing what relief might be contained in its package of behavioral, educational, and pharmaceutical interventions. Our response was just as scientific as the data we were offered. The cost of following the wrong path was never understood until we had done the damage by escalating Jack's symptoms, experiencing the negative consequences of poorly tested drugs and playing pin the tail on the diagnosis. Obstructions to normal growth slowly unfolded over the course of Jack's infancy and throughout his early school years. Problems were manifested in intolerance for the rigors of traditional learning, speech and language processing deficits, and incomprehensible behavior patterns that dismayed and frightened everyone in his company. Despite our attempts to achieve clarity, so little was understood about what was actually wrong with our son. As a result, we spent much of Jack's early life trying to out run the odds-makers who knew something was wrong, struggled to classify the deficits, and predicted nothing but trouble for the future.

There are many boys with quirky minds, marked by the social and emotional differences that set them apart from the merely cranky, uncooperative children who are likely to outgrow their behaviors as late teenage and adult years dull the ragged edges with maturity. Jack may never walk the road to normalcy. For much of his life he has had to design a path with his own road map. It was never easy for him, and sometimes it was impossible for us to follow.

Our journey is not rare, but recording it in these pages may be unusual. Secrecy has been a convenient cloak to hide the missteps and mistakes of families living with rare, troubling disorders. It is tempting to pull these pages back inside a magic cape, holding them out of sight. I might still want the protection of anonymity and denial, except for two things.

First, this story is true.

Second, we are not alone in the struggle with our difficult, sometimes destructive child, whom we love and have tried to help. Tens of thousands of families are living in silence and regret. Like us, they are afraid to acknowledge how hard they have fought to parent different, uncompromising children. These parents are frightened at the prospect of living indefinitely without the key to the puzzle that keeps them trapped and isolated from the world. As we have done, I believe these families must also deal with a realistic, but sad recognition: one child with severe emotional disabilities sucks up the resources meant to nurture an entire family, leaving siblings, friends, and parents without the hope that can lead you to another day.

Throughout our son's life, we made the choice to tolerate behaviors so erratic and distressing that nearly everyone in our life questioned our sanity or abandoned our company. Our family made a slow, often painful voyage to understanding what our love for Jack would endure and what we could not abide. Like thousands of other parents made mute by their child's unspecified problems, I waited for the day when our son would be "better," sacrificing years meant to be lived in the present.

Like a Mobius strip that runs in loops that never meet, we got lost in the stultifying tangle of testing and evaluating unspecified diagnoses. I hoped each procedure would confirm that my son was ill, and we grieved when we came up empty because there were no tools to make him better. In the process I learned many things about pediatric neurology and brain function as I sought answers to Jack's perplexing behavior.

Emotional disturbance in boys is one of the fastest-growing diagnoses within the special education world. The number of diagnoses of mild to serious emotional problems has risen consistently during the last decade. Boys with emotional disabilities far outnumber classified girls. Often, more specific labeling attends problems experienced by girls. There are many reasons for this anomaly, including later diagnoses and the range of eating and anxiety disorders that appear to affect girls more frequently. Many boys harboring emotional issues are not identified until the consequence of their disability (school failure, violence, drug use) outs the problem. By the time parents are calling the lawyers and severing deeply troubled relationships, the cause of the breakdown in normal growth and development is no longer the focus.

Understanding what has made boys like Jack so different from his peers has forced experts and parents to rely on observations and anecdotal data. If my child is not appropriately contained within another protocol of autism or conduct disorder, but he still needs substantial intervention to stay in school, a diagnosis of emotional disability may do the honors. Over time, the catchall school-based label has held in its grip children whose behavior ranges from mildly inappropriate to psychotic. Others are almost inert from disinterest and lack of engaging with the world around them. There are many boys like Jack who dazzle and dismay with "scattershot" genius in art, music, or mathematics. At seventeen, Jack could operate nearly anything powered by an engine. Yet he could not cope with the dizzying number of pages contained in a telephone book to look up a number or write an address on an envelope.

Boys with emotional disabilities may be preparing for employment or for lives of dependence. They may share friends, family, and intimacy, or they may shun all personal contact, isolated from perceived hostility. Their worlds turn on a dime. What made sense yesterday may have no place in the challenges of today. Tomorrow is not only a new day, it can be the first day on a path to be followed for weeks or months, or never to be taken again.

Fixing Jack became a family activity, like other families immersed themselves in soccer or music. Evaluations, special camps, programs, parenting education classes, isolation, lying, cheerleading, and ignoring what was right in front of us were all strategies we used at one time or another. It was a disheartening path for our family. Always there was the promise of change and peace; always the uncertainty and the guilt for participating in a recipe for disaster regardless of the skills and qualifications of the professionals leading us down the only path they knew.

In time I would learn that the heart of the definition of a child's dysfunction was often betrayed in the emphasis or academic skill of the definer. Psychiatrists saw trauma; psychologists sorted out the impact of relationships; pediatricians alerted parents to atypical patterns in health and development. Neuroscientists conversed in synapses and serotonin. And they were all right at one time or another during the perplexing to terrifying moments in our family journey.

As is true for many families who struggle with differently behaved children, our son is adopted. Brought into our life at his birth, I assisted his birth mother in the delivery room and was the first person to hold Jack before passing him to my husband. With limited birth family health history, we don't know if other blood relatives lived through emotional trauma or mental illness, or possessed remarkable genius. It isn't clear why many adopted children inherit such complex social and emotional difficulties. But adopted boys and girls are disproportionately represented among children with problems that impede natural growth and development.

Our son was born in the United States in a sophisticated hospital. His birth mother was healthy and reported no complications during her pregnancy. Did our birth mother use drugs or alcohol during her pregnancy? Random drug testing was required in order for her to receive living expenses and medical services, but that is not a guarantee of sobriety, as anyone who reads the sports pages knows. She had good prenatal care. There was no trauma before or after a routine cesarean delivery. She assured us repeatedly that she was taking care of herself and of our baby.

We had waited for an adoption for nearly two years, an untidy emotional roller coaster. With our history of losing babies, the new terrors of adoption quelled to silence aggressive questioning about illicit drugs and past family history. Two other potential adoptions had already fallen through by the time we got to Jack. It seemed counterintuitive to raise hostile questions with our birth mother, so I never pressed.

The attending pediatrician said to us before we left the hospital, "You have a perfect baby." Did he lie to us so we wouldn't renege on the adoption? Were we ignorant of the protections available against the life of chaos we chose? We just don't know. We did know what it was like to wait for the silence of a baby's heartbeat. We were not losing this baby, and that's all we thought about.

During the journey of Jack's life, I worked to snatch normalcy from a suitcase packed with every congenital or traumatic disability from autism to zinc deficiency. Each fear or possibility was raised and investigated, tested and rejected until the experts had nothing left to say except, "I don't know what's wrong with him," if they were brave, or "More research is happening every day," if they were not.

My fearless psychiatrist was willing to push the envelope, questioning the child experts and looking for any answers that might quiet my mind and ease our desperation about Jack's multiplying problems. After years of reading Jack's varied and numerous evaluations, this trusted doctor finally diagnosed our son with "Jack's syndrome," a disorder all our own that cut across more authoritative, but far less accurate diagnoses of mental or physical disorders. Our family has used it ever since. This small slice of made-up certainty brought some peace I never found in searching the system for another truth.

Medicine, educational plans and interventions, and persistent evaluations all left us empty-handed and hurting sooner or later. Eventually, we stopped hoping for the answers that would make Jack whole. In fact, science and all its cohorts became a wall to scale without the ropes. That's when I turned away from the quest to understand "what in the world is wrong with Jack" and moved toward the task of making a family that would survive our son's demons and offer a place for love and memories to grow.

CHAPTER FOUR

BLAST THE BRIDGE

Children seemed to have built-in bullshit detectors, instantly spotting the adult who would leave them without a backward glance as soon as escape is possible. Sitting with a child born with AIDS, underweight and anxious from cocaine withdrawal, I once watched as a national health official reached out for the boy's hand as the television cameras flashed. Never quite connecting, the man turned away when the press was finished. My little charge looked up and said, "He bye-byed me." Indeed he did.

My professional choices led me to children's advocacy, finally in New York State government, where I spent most of my time with sick babies born with cocaine addictions, pregnant teens, and achingly dysfunctional families that abused each other every day. I logged hundreds of hours at homeless shelters, neo-natal care units, and protective housing for aggressive juveniles and abused children. Perhaps like many others doing similar work, I thought I could be part of changing a broken and blind system that accepted as inevitable the failure of a staggering number of children and families. Over time, I knew my impact was brief and unsatisfactory. The problems were overwhelming and there may not be enough resources in the universe to erase the all scars of such fragile people. So, while I was with these young boys and girls and their parents, I did the one thing I knew I could do; I took every opportunity available to make someone smile.

Colleagues teased me for years that my pleasure and success with children was a result of my joy at getting down on the rug to play trucks and "Blast the Bridge," a deliciously chaotic game of my own invention. The point was to build two towers out of soft-surface building materials such as cardboard, newspaper, sweaters, and blankets, plastic blocks, anything. Once the columns were barely supporting their own weight, a makeshift plank was laid on top to connect the bridge. Of course, everything immediately toppled, offering a sea of soft jetsam for rolling and playing. Once or twice, child-care workers had to insist that I stop this frenzied routine. The game apparently overexcited the children for an entire day.

But babies were not to be a part of the picture for Sam and me. We always thought there would be time. When we ran out of time—somewhere in my late thirties—fate or whatever controls successful pregnancies abandoned the cause. So, at age forty-one, after nineteen years of marriage, three miscarriages, and one ectopic pregnancy that nearly killed me, the ache for children was so intense that we threw ourselves into the chronically terrifying prospect of private adoption. Would we find a child? Would the birth mother change her mind? Would the baby be healthy?

After months of waiting, we found ourselves standing outside of the door to our birth mother's Southern California apartment. With a suddenness that startled me into a backward fall, the apartment door swung open, and there she was.

Hannah was nineteen years old when she was pregnant with our son. Abandoned by her mother at age twelve to loving grandparents, Hannah was a sensitive, intelligent young woman. Tall, blonde, and beautiful, she was five months pregnant on the day we met. She had shared with us the results of a recent ultrasound, so we knew we were having a boy and had already named him Jack. We were joyfully pulled inside. Hannah spoke rapidly, simultaneously showing us the apartment, introducing us to her roommate, and saying we were much more attractive than our pictures and asking why we hadn't sent something different.

The stream of words halted for a moment, and I found my voice. "Different how, what should we have sent?" The excitement and fatigue of the cross-country flight was playing havoc with my emotions. Hot tears gathered behind my eyes. Looking at me, she quickly apologized.

"I like the picture," she rushed to tell me, horrified at my tears. "I just mean you are prettier, younger-looking. Nicer. You sound so different on the phone, fun and loving."

Standing at her bedroom door, I saw our picture placed on the bedside table. The putative parents smiling forced smiles and screaming, "Choose us" like some manic entry in a talent contest. Had she put it there that morning, or had it been there since we sent it to her, months before? I immediately regretted my suspicions and wondered instead, "What does she think about when she looks at us? Does she say good night and good morning?" Books were stacked from the floor to the table, the saltines and the ginger ale near the clock radio.

"I passed over you once in the book they gave me to look through for parents for my baby. I got to choose my adoptive parents. I liked what you wrote about wanting a child. I liked the things you do; I like how long you've been married. Nineteen years. As old as I am."

"You are three years older than my mother," Hannah added as an afterthought, glancing toward me to gauge my reaction.

"Is that a good thing?" I laughed, recovering from my initial anxiety but feeling for just a moment that we were adopting our grandson.

"Yeah, that's a great thing. My mom is really a nut, but she could have grown up, she just didn't. I figured you are both grown-ups. I want grown-up parents for our son."

"I don't know much about my father," Hannah continued her life story. "My sister has a different father. My grandparents raised me. I can't have a baby. Well, I am having a baby, but I can't raise a kid."

These sentences rushed out in a staccato confession, and then she was spent, flopping back on the bed, big belly swelling out of her middle. Remarkably long legs, capped by feet clad in ballet slippers, touched the floor. It was the first time I had looked below her neck. I was afraid to confront our son in Hannah's body.

"We weren't given a book of pictures," I told her slowly, wondering if we would have picked her from a pregnancy lineup.

Private adoption worked for us, and after all these years I remain a strong supporter of bringing adoption out from behind the secret curtain and into the twenty-first century. Everyone involved deserves the opportunity to share as little or as much information as they choose. We had been advised by some people to use false names and a bogus address. We were forthright in our approach to everyone involved; I don't think we knew any better. Scars running deep through my miscarriages and the grief that left me out of the biological baby market made me want to declare absolutely that I wanted this baby. Sam and I jumped right in with the whole truth complete with real phone numbers and addresses that could be tracked down today.

Sam turned away from the small bedroom, leading us back to the living room. I took a last look. Our picture and the books were the only personal touches here. My recent gift, Maya Angelou's *I Know Why the Caged Bird Sings*, sat on top of the pile. I couldn't see the other titles.

After one or two false starts, Hannah asked Sam if he would mind if she and I took a walk. Handing him the Sunday New York Times and airplane-size bottles of Dewar's, Hannah directed me to the door. Sam eyed the tiny drinks with gratitude.

"Walk on the beach with me?" She was heading down the city block to the Pacific Ocean.

Once we were taking in the sights of the beach, Hannah asked anxiously, "Do you think he's upset? I don't know too many men his age."

"Sam? No, no, he's not upset, not with those props," I teased, gently. "He wants you to be comfortable with us, with him. He's fine." I'm not sure what she wanted to know about my comfortable, comforting husband.

Looking down at her swollen belly, Hannah touched her baby bulge.

"How do you know if you love him?"

"Sam?" I asked.

"No, how do you know if you love the baby? I know you love Sam. People don't stay married as long as you've been married if they don't love each other." Hannah was confident about our marriage.

"I just know I love him. I don't know why. That's the truth." I wanted to reassure her, but I had nothing to say that sounded more believable. I couldn't meet her eyes, and I hoped that my inadequate confessions of love were enough.

Walking across the beach, Hannah struggled with shifting sand and the uneven weight of her pregnancy. Breathless, I tried to keep up with her loping gait. For the first time she laughed, realizing I had been left in the wake of the stride that her five-foot-ten-inch body allowed. We looped arms, trying to even out the speed. Battling our differing walking styles was clumsy, and we soon sank down on the warm sand.

The sun started its descent, changing the sky from blue to tangerine, and then to indigo, cut sporadically with blazing yellow.

"I didn't love Jack's birth father. I didn't know him. He was cute, nice. But it wasn't a relationship. It just happened."

"You got pregnant. It doesn't matter that you didn't love him. It matters that you know we love this child."

"Will you love Jack always, forever, no matter what?" Hannah stared out into the wide Pacific Ocean, waiting.

Looking at her, I was stunned by the beauty of her face in the sunlight. Holding her breath, listening for my answer, she looked like a model maintaining her pose until the crew got the lighting just right.

I promised, "I'll love him always, forever, no matter what."

I put my hand on her belly, tentatively touching. Jack kicked my hand.

"Here's his butt," she identified a rounded bump. "I told him about you. I told him he'd have a daddy, too, a good one."

"Let's go back," I suggested, suddenly anxious to be with Jack's waiting daddy. "Are you okay?" I pulled her from her seated position on the sand, losing my balance beneath her height and weight. We held on to each other, hugging tight for support.

"I'm fine." Hannah smiled, taking me through the looking glass to the first shadow of my son's face.

Much later, as Jack's curiosity about his adoption grew, so did his knowledge of the powerful weapon possessed by adopted children: "You're not my real mother, and I don't have to do anything you say," was lobbed at me for the first time when he was six years old. I had anticipated this reprimand from the moment he formed some understanding of the concept of adoption. It was still a punch to the solar plexus.

Hannah and Jack may yet find each other. I don't know how I'll feel, but I hope I can find some measure of the gentle affection she has shown me.

Chapter Five

Class Act

Monday, June 12, 1989, standing in an elevator at Cedars-Sinai Medical Center in Beverly Hills, California, Sam and I strained to get to the fourth floor, repeatedly pushing at the "Up" button. We were scared, disbelieving, and so unaware of the surroundings that we didn't see Milton Berle holding open the door to the elevator. His signature unlit cigar was in his hand. Elegant in the early morning gloom, he stood patiently, waiting for us to enter as the doors opened and shut again when we didn't move fast enough.

Smiling, he drawled at us, "What's the hurry—you're going to hurt yourself!" This last comment was directed at my awkward jump through the closing steel doors.

"We're having a baby and we're late," I said, doing a rapid two-step of confusion and haste before hitting my head on the back wall of the elevator. Mr. Berle held out his hand and pulled me away from the wall as the elevator lifted us away from the lobby.

"You look remarkably good." I laughed and relaxed, explaining we were adopting a baby boy who would be born in a few minutes. Mr. Berle asked my name, and I gave him my business card before he left us at the surgical recovery floor, telling us he had an "old trouper" to visit. When I told Hannah about our chance meeting, she said she had never heard of Milton Berle but thought her grandmother might know him. In what I still think of as a class act, she received a dozen congratulatory roses that afternoon with "Uncle Milty" scribbled across a blue card from the Cedars-Sinai's flower shop.

The previous day, a mild California earthquake had thrown everyone into a panic, altering birthing schedules. The maternity floor nurse explained this to Hannah at least a dozen times. "This happens sometimes when there's an earthquake. The quake changes blood pressure or biorhythms or something. Don't worry about it," she said brushing aside Hannah's impatience to get this birth over with. More at ease with the biorhythms on the East Coast, I marveled that it was possible to consider mild an event that involved two plates of rock buried deep in the earth, scraping together and causing all manner of havoc. Throughout the long day, Sam, Hannah, and I took turns on the bed and the two Beverly Hills issue chrome-and-leather hospital chairs. We dressed the oversized wheelchair in a green hospital cap and blue scrubs, tying a kerchief around its back panel and christening him "Toro." When an orderly came to reclaim the chair, we waved good-bye and told our new friend to be in touch, laughing with the hysteria of fatigue.

Hannah was in pain from time to time, and her labor wasn't moving toward a baby, a fact that became a concern to all of us. Attending Lamaze classes for weeks before the birth, I had prepared as a coach for a single mother in my hometown. But there wasn't any role for me here. Doctors wandered through the room checking machines and the wires to Hannah's body.

Routine examinations determined insufficient dilation. Converting centimeters confused me when I was calm and filled me with anxiety as I tried to work through what the doctors were saying. It was silly because I didn't know the magic number on either scale, but I kept trying to do the math, because I was not in charge of anything else.

Long after midnight, Sam and I made another run for ice chips, the only thing Hannah had been allowed for eighteen hours. We gave up pretending the shaved ice was KFC hash browns or sushi, deciding it was no longer funny to a weary young woman who was three days overdue and not progressing. Telling her to rest, I kissed her, and we left for the hotel. Her obstetrician was on the down elevator. He warned us that because this was an adoption he wouldn't wait much longer.

"What do you mean?" I asked wondering if there were some weird time limits in which adoptions must occur before hospitals withdraw their support. I was really tired.

"Just that when a young women has decided on adoption, we don't prolong labor if a C-section can be done safely," he explained.

"Oh, that's good, that's a good thing," I babbled at him, but he was out the door. Sam and I stopped for a cheeseburger on our way to the hotel. We felt guilty eating in front of Hannah and took turns hiding our consumption of coffee and bagels throughout the day.

The call came from the obstetrician at 5:15 A.M. Neither of us was sleeping.

"I'm not waiting any longer. Be here in thirty minutes if you plan to be in on this birth," he announced.

Twenty-six minutes to the hospital, two minutes in the elevator, three minutes to scrub, thirty minutes more for the C-section, and Jack was in my arms. Holding our baby filled me with an unfamiliar passion for possession, as I stood awestruck beside the woman who had given him life. Sam was soon with me for the silver nitrate drops and to begin the baby's bath. I was in love.

The C-section explained the smooth pink skin and spared him the unnaturally elongated head, but only something divinely inspired could have imagined that face. Huge blue eyes and a nose that was sure to grow straight were set in translucent skin. My little finger traced a perfect bee-sting mouth. Dimples we would wait for as smiles were learned now formed small bruised shadows in the cleft of his chin and cheek. He was perfect.

Our new family left for home two days later in a 737 across the country.

When the nurse let us know that the taxi for the airport had arrived, I climbed into Hannah's bed and took her in my arms. Sam sat down next to both of us, holding my hand and brushing Hannah's long blond hair back from her forehead. Jack lay sleeping in the curve of Hannah's elbow while her hand beat a soft tap-tap against Jack's back. As she kissed our baby for the last time, the rhythm of her hand ceased, but I heard the echo keeping time with my heartbeat. With all of the things we had to say to each other, I was silent, memorizing that tapping sequence, positive this detail would be important. Rising from the bed, I took our son and began to make the same motion against his back with my hand. She reached up to cover my hand with her own. Neither of us spoke a word.

Hannah's gift is still beyond my comprehension. After I held Jack that first time in the delivery room, I could not have unfolded my arms, offered him to another, and said good-bye.

I have known that kind of grace just this once.

CHAPTER SIX

ORGANIC APPLESAUCE AND
THE BIG BANG THEORY OF DISABILITY

Those first hours as a family were spent flying thousands of miles across country, giddy and sleep deprived. As we looked for our seats once we were on board the plane, the steward stopped us and quietly explained that babies must be three weeks old before the airline allows them to fly.

"He is," I lied.

"No, he isn't," argued the steward. "I have four kids, and he was born yesterday."

"It was two days ago, actually," I corrected. Sam pulled out the preliminary adoption papers and was about to launch into a well-formed lawyerly argument on permissions and special circumstances. I took the shorter route. I started to cry.

The steward made a quick decision after looking us over. "Go to first class, sit in the bulkhead seats, and keep the baby out of sight until after takeoff." He smiled and was gone. After takeoff, our co-conspirator brought us glasses of straight scotch on the correct assumption I wasn't breastfeeding, and we could probably use it.

Throughout the flight there was a steady stream of admirers, and finally, a visit from the captain. "I want to see the stowaway," he demanded. My husband pulled aside the hospital's blue blanket, removed an oversized hat, and presented him for viewing. Jack seemed to lean into the captain's voice and formally greeted him with a hearty burp. "My youngest passenger ever is already complaining about the airline food." Jack got his silver wings, and the long flight eventually brought us home.

The airport was chaotic. Friends who managed to figure out when we would arrive besieged us with welcoming words and demands to see the baby. Neither Sam nor I was prepared for the crowd. Voices speaking right in front of me seemed to reach me through a long tube, echoing around the steel and linoleum decor decking out the arrival gate. For the first time in more years than I could remember, I experienced a primal need to see my mother. Both of my parents were moving through the crowd, my father irritated that he had been made to wait in a line of sorts to see his grandson, and my mother smiling her worried smile. She reached for Jack, and I handed him to her, acutely aware that my arms were frozen in the cradling position after twelve hours of holding on for dear life.

We were home.

Memories of the next few weeks are blunted by sleep deprivation and constant self-doubt: Was I feeding him enough or too much? Why didn't he ever keep his left foot in the blanket? Was his leg hurting, or was his foot growing improperly? Should I check on him every twenty minutes or more often? Sam and I rotated feeding schedules at midnight, 3:00 A.M. and 6:15 A.M., heating the bottle and trekking back to his room. Nobody slept except Jack.

After six weeks, my eyes flew wide open and the normally accurate bedside clock displayed an impossible 7:15 A.M. on the dial. The last time I looked it was midnight.

"Oh my God, he's dead," I said.

Flailing legs carried me across the hall. In my panic, I threw myself into the room, bumping his crib, breaking my little toe, and screaming in pain. This last bit of acrobatics brought Sam at warp speed. We found a sleeping baby, happy that his growing stomach had managed to store enough fuel for the night. I checked on his left foot, still outside the blanket. It seemed to be growing just fine. My toe healed in a couple of weeks.

During the first few months of Jack's life, he and I were happy tramps—sleeping in, eating, and laughing. In these weeks of self-indulgence and serenity, I was busy savoring the changing landscape of Jack's face. Colleagues called me, still present in the hectic life of my formerly frantic job. Asked what I was doing, I was embarrassed to say I was rocking in a chair and looking at my son, rocking and looking and planning the future together. So I usually said I was making organic applesauce (something I never did), but then someone asked for a sample so I switched to talking about the laundry.

Jack had his normal moments of baby distress. He cried and refused to be comforted and slept all day and wanted to play all night. He had ear infections and projectile vomiting and a pucker in the middle of his forehead that I took to be consternation with my poor mind-reading skills. For my part, I was anxious, exasperated, patient, sympathetic, and bone-crushingly tired all before nine in the morning.

The wonder of Jack's presence in our lives never faded, but soon there were new and more challenging things to wonder about.

Was there a moment of epiphany when Jack's disability was suddenly illuminated? I think we crept away from normal on a slow and bumpy road littered with contradictory data. One day we were a new family, making our way. Soon we were on our knees, struggling to cope with a rapid descent into parenting hell.

At the onset of Jack's disabilities, I hadn't the slightest notion of what was happening. If I could understand what triggered the two-hour tantrum I could not soothe, could I remove whatever "it" was and heal my son? If we could pinpoint that cataclysmic event that moved us off the path to "typical child," could we have taken the first step in a giant redo?

If only.

If only we knew which one of the hundred million genetic or environmental combinations fired or misfired, could we retrace our steps to that certain place and try again? Rewire the connection and snuff out the explosive flame? This was my big bang theory of disability—not a very scientific approach, but comforting in the idea that I could control the maelstrom of Jack's unpredictability and avoid the truth that all three of us were seriously out of sync with the rest of the families that were part of our world. After Jack's birth, as most new parents do, we connected with friends and neighbors who had recently become new parents, some who were veterans of two or three children. Grateful for new mom friends sharing the same shifting schedules and adapting to a similar scarcity of social opportunities, I bonded quickly; glad to have play dates and adult coffee time.

Jack was so perfect physically that I was probably less attentive to any deficits lurking in nascent language and coping skills. He was crawling, sitting up, and making sounds that passed for early language. He was also sleeping fourteen hours a day, and although he walked right on time at eleven months, he had limited fine-motor skills, unable to hold a spoon or a small cup handle. I was content to hear "He's the most beautiful baby I've ever seen," a frequent claim from the group of admirers that gathered everywhere we went. Total strangers suggested contacting baby modeling agencies. I was Narcissus, satisfied to relax in the reflective pools of his deep blue eyes.

What now seems most likely is that the gap between our son and other babies was always there. We noticed it first as a tiny crack. This fissure strained and splintered as he grew, and the things that didn't quite fit pushed against the boundaries of developmental expectations. Then the gap widened, and the differences spilled out in a swirling pool of uncertainty, fear, and confusion.

I do remember the day we stopped looking for normal.

CHAPTER SEVEN

CHANGELING

There was a place within Jack that I could never touch. I couldn't get close to the place where children grow and thrive without dangerously veering into extreme behaviors that typified my son's growth and development. Confronting this information was a task I avoided for months until I no longer could feign ignorance.

Our habit was to read in the afternoon, usually after Jack's nap. Virginia Lee Burton's *Mike Mulligan and His Steam Shovel* was a favorite, and one day he picked it out of the pile on his bookcase, offered it to me, and climbed on my lap. Jack often grew restless after three or four pages, but I could usually redirect his attention by touching the side of his face, gently pulling his head back to the book on my lap. Kissing the top of his head, I felt him slowly turn in the direction of my voice.

Suddenly still, the eyes meeting mine weren't the cheerful summer-blue eyes that were the centerpiece of his gorgeous face. Black and vacant, these eyes swept his surroundings until his face became pinched with discontent and anxiety. Pushing me away, he dropped to the floor. Shaking off my attempts to touch him, he seemed to droop with disinterest whenever I came into his line of vision. Settling in front of a box of trucks, he played with a slow, restless energy, never glancing in my direction, his back rigid and unwelcoming.

I went back to the chair where he had last smiled at me, sat down, and stared at him. The background of cooing and first language noises that had been the soundtrack to my days was gone. The silence was claustrophobic. Soft sounds of small trucks being moved over the carpet was all there was. Blood surged through my body, each vessel expanding until I was stilled with breathless terror. Frozen in my chair, my muscles ached from the effort to calm my body. I sat silently screaming for Jack to return. Fifteen minutes passed while I watched his precise disconnectedness, fully aware that he was not with me in the room.

Without warning, the spell was broken, and Jack was back. Turning toward my chair, he looked surprised to see me there. Smiling and laughing, his arms reached out to me. His words "Uppy, uppy" broke the silence. Flooded with relief, I pulled him into my arms and held on tight, while he bubbled and laughed.

Throughout the day, my panic would rise and subside as I scoured child-care books and drank multiple cups of coffee. Jack played happily, climbing over my books, happy to be hugged and cuddled whenever I took a break. Information that came close to describing what I had experienced with him was included under chapters about failure to thrive and developmental disability, and certainly autism. Finally, I concluded I would not find the words I was searching for, words telling me this bizarre and frightening behavior was just a fluke and right on schedule for a twenty-six-month-old child.

I put the child-care books away on the top shelf in the kitchen. Then I told myself I was sleep deprived, and I was imagining the intensity of the moment. Now I know that this afternoon episode was the first step in facing a jumbled set of feelings and suspicions that had already haunted me for many months.

Something was very wrong with my son.

Once I opened the floodgates of suspicion, the warning signs were everywhere. Why did he stare, rigid and unblinking at the ceiling fan without making a sound? Why did he sleep so much? Other parents were envious of his sleep marathons, but I was edgy and nervous, wanting to hold and care for my child instead of watching him sleep in the crib. Efforts to awaken him terrified him. Instead of welcoming his release from the crib, he'd arch his body away from me, screaming at a decibel point that nearly shattered my senses. I would lay him down again and almost hear his unspoken dismissal pushing me out of his room. I knew this behavior fit under the category of autism or other developmental disorders. I read books, consulted the Internet, investigated potential evaluations, and waited.

My pediatrician was already aware of our concerns but didn't have enough proof to substantiate or deny any of my fears. My calls about the sleeping were treated with proper respect but not taken very seriously:

"When he sleeps for twenty-four hours straight, call me back. Until then, count your lucky stars."

I didn't feel lucky. I felt estranged from my son. His constant sleeping heightened our isolation from each other, as though his nocturnal habits were a way of keeping me at bay. I asked my mother, who assured me he was content and happy. I tried to explain to other mothers that I knew something was

41

wrong but couldn't name my fears for Jack. Friends were concerned because I was so unhappy, but they didn't know how to reassure me. Most friends tried to lighten my mood by expressing their envy over my quiet and contented child. They didn't often see the two-hour temper tantrums. I was careful to hide this behavior, racing from the playground or the party as soon as I sensed Jack's fragile control was starting to slip. If I was unwise and blurted out my suspicions on the playground, mothers with two and three children reacted as though I needed more to do.

Some days, Jack's behavior floated on the edge of normalcy for twelve out of sixteen hours, and I celebrated the quiet trip to the grocery store or the relaxed afternoon with a friend. There were so many explanations for a cranky, discontented child, but these held less meaning for me each time I went through them in my head: He's teething, he's allergic to rice cereal, he needs special detergent, he has a vitamin deficiency. These were the maladies I prayed for. I wanted some guardian of frenzied children to pick a problem, name it for me, and tell me when it would end.

As Jack began to walk, growing into a toddler, I had to acknowledge that he seemed very different. He didn't respond to simple directions, he was unconcerned if I lost sight of him, undaunted by finding himself in the company of strangers. Each day he seemed to experiment with a new form of recklessness, a pursuit that he would never leave behind.

Not everyone responded with fear and dread at the changes in Jack.

"Such a little man," said his grandfather, noting he wasn't afraid of anything and rarely cried after childhood falls. Tottering close to the edge of the path, eager to stand and sway at the top of the open staircase, Jack was ever defiant of the deep end of the pool.

Our swim club was a place we could be successful as a family. Jack's loud outbursts and frantic movements from the locker room to the baby pool and back caused just a few raised eyebrows. There were, after all, many spirited toddlers, and Jack seemed to be more contained in the wide-open space. But when he slipped the firm grasp that helped me believe he was bound to my side, he sometimes charged toward the twelve-foot end of the pool, hurling himself underwater absent the fear that can insulate the hesitant swimmer from danger.

Twice I found myself catapulting across the pavement, diving in, and pulling him out as his body sank contentedly to the bottom. Both times he seemed surprised and a little disturbed to be interrupted in his watery descent. After the third marathon run to pull him from the pool, the lifeguards, unprepared for his speed and agility, pulled me aside, asking me to keep a closer watch. Unwilling to seek their understanding, I retreated to the privacy of home.

On the trip home, Jack scrutinized each tree and road sign as though these wonders had been introduced just for his enjoyment. My words, "Mommy was really scared when you ran away and jumped into the big pool" got his attention momentarily. From his car seat in the back, he met my eyes in the rearview mirror, a remote almost lifeless stare searching out the sound of my voice. With an effort, I pulled my attention back to the highway. Sitting in the backseat was a changeling occupying my child's car seat. Finding no good purpose in this disconcerting retreat into thin air, it was easier for me to believe he was gone and would be back soon.

Sam and I began to talk more often about Jack's behavior. Instead of coming home at the end of the day and engaging his son in play and hugs, he began asking, "How's Jack?" and then seemed to watch me for signs of the kind of day it had been, unerringly reading my face.

"What happened?" he would ask while loosening his tie in the doorway, tilting his head sideways as he does when he's sure of trouble. Often I reported what I thought were small things: temper tantrums that lasted two hours, disregard of instructions causing me to lose him at the grocery store.

"It's not small," Sam said one day after I downplayed Jack's flight through the local mall that eventually required help from security before I found him hiding in the ladies' room. "You're getting immune to his behavior—making excuses for him."

"It's fine; I just had a bad day. Can't you let it drop? Jack is okay."

"Jack is wearing you out, wearing us down. There aren't any good days. When are you going to give it up and get some help?"

His worry didn't reach me. I blew up, angrier than I ever remember being with my life partner.

"Go away," I shouted at him. "If you can't handle this, just go away." Pushing away Sam when he challenged my capacity to deal with whatever Jack dished out was a pattern I set early in our family life. This behavior ultimately would not support our marriage and threatened the daily connection between us. I denied the difficulties we were facing, and Sam retreated when I sidestepped his love and good sense.

Coping with Jack's behavior distorted my reason; soon, I believed, I would run out of time or room in my heart to hold both Sam and Jack. Real damage would be done before I understood this faulty version of "I am strong, and you are getting in the way of my saving our son." There was no reason for doubting Sam's love for me and his commitment to his son. I didn't need a reason, I just let my own misgivings narrow my world until trust became unfamiliar and then unwelcome.

Keeping the bad news under wraps would control Jack's fate. Glued to his side, without the company of other moms or toddlers, I tried to stave off the discovery of how different our life was becoming from the mom and dad exhausted by children who pushed the limits of daily peace as their children grew and gained confidence. We were losing our grip on the happy family world as the long shadow of a disability I could not name closed in and eclipsed our light.

Whatever in the world was wrong with Jack, I knew I could no longer pretend that his disability was only a short respite from normalcy. Chaos, disconnection, and despair—this was our normal, and it wasn't anywhere near where normal lives.

CHAPTER EIGHT

RUNNING WITH SCISSORS

By age four, Jack was separating from his peers and quickly widening the gap. They were potty trained; he had no interest in mastering this skill. They were speaking; he used a disturbing economy of words. They were anxious to please; he was intent on having his own way, regardless of the consequences. I harvested only the hopeful signs, only the instances where he resembled his peers. I gorged on the smallest achievement— each new word he spoke and the brief flashes of similarity to other children.

There were many days when Jack raced from unpredictable to horrifying in a few tenacious steps. Finally, the day arrived when Jack lost the battle with any sort of normalcy, and I lost my energetic capacity for delusional thinking about my son's delays and deficits. This tipping point came in the middle of a sunny October day made for sweet-tart cider and a child's laughter carried on the wind of changing seasons.

As fall spilled into early winter, families began that annual New England tradition of the harvest. Apple orchards and pumpkin patches were especially favorite destinations for the preschoolers in my neighborhood. Recalling pleasant memories of my own occasional odysseys away from the cities that housed us, I saw this foray into hayrides and cider donuts as a chance to be a part of a group of happy moms and kids. We would have a normal day.

Dressed for the cold, we arrived alone at a local orchard, giving the bus a pass "just in case" an early retreat to our car was necessary. We were always alone, but I explained it by telling him this would be more fun than a noisy, smelly bus. He seemed delighted with the open spaces and the thrill of the search, as twenty-five other young children culled through fields of precut miniature pumpkins waiting for little hands to scoop them up.

The festivities involved capturing pumpkins for painting and decorating with simple felt hats, big buttons, and a gallon of glue. Jack had no interest in altering the natural state of his pumpkin and began to cry when a considerate worker cut off the stem to make room for a witch's hat. I rescued the pumpkin and told him it was beautiful just as it was. Watching with trained eyes, I saw his growing anxiety, fed by his distress at his now deformed pumpkin.

"Why don't we take a walk and get a donut?" I said with too much enthusiasm. He ignored me and made one of those sudden movements I was always trying to anticipate, going for the craft helper with a blunt-edged child's scissors he found on the table.

"No, Jack!"

He continued his assault, not hearing my voice.

"Stop it, Jack."

His full-blown rage carried him past the point of my flimsy control. Now screaming at a pitch that unnerved the other children, I sought and held the helper's eyes. Her face told the whole story. Who was this child intent on thrusting a scissors through her chest? Quickly stepping around the ménage of helpers and parents who had gathered to assist, I retrieved the scissors and pulled his arms from her waist.

I grabbed him from behind, and Jack stretched out his body making a rigid slat so it was impossible to hold on to him. Summoning up strength from some deep place, I pulled him under my one arm and tried to keep his hands still with the other. I headed for the door, making ineffectual apologies along the way. Other moms quieted their children, casting down their eyes, but not before I saw that mixture of pity and surprise that exposed every doubt I had about my son. I refused well-meant assistance intended to help me get him into the car. We finally made the long drive home in total silence. Jack was unaware that anything was wrong with our outing. We had been there forty-seven minutes.

I called the pediatrician as soon as we walked through the door.

CHAPTER NINE

BREAKING THE CODE OF DISABILITY

Jack's pediatrician was not the "everything will be fine, just let things settle down" variety. He had seven children of his own, and he listened to me, always asking me what I thought before he gave me his opinion. I liked him. Active listening is a rare quality in any person and is especially rare in healthcare professionals listening to moms. Some pediatric and disability professionals I talked to about Jack were the best multitasking people I have ever come across; updating charts, looking at another report, writing a prescription, and nodding at comments while never making eye contact. I'd never left Jack's pediatrician feeling incompetent.

Explaining the details of the afternoon in the pumpkin patch and the other clues that worried and frightened me, I put my fears into words. The doctor had heard some of these concerns in the past. Although not dismissive, he had counseled patience. He sensed my new urgency, listened quietly, and occasionally looked at Jack, who was trying to unscrew the heating vent in his consulting office. Although he asked him to stop several times, Jack went ahead with his work as though he hadn't heard.

"Jack." He raised his voice. Jack stopped and looked at his doctor. "I asked you to please stop."

"No," Jack said. "I won't." I picked up Jack, trying to interest him in my keys. He slipped out of my arms and was back at the vent in an instant.

"Let him go. I'm more interested in how often he complies when you ask him to do something."

A strangled giggle-cry burst from my mouth as I fought to hold back the tears. "He almost never complies. He almost never does anything he is asked to do. He's not potty trained, doesn't speak unless all tantrums fail, doesn't follow simple commands, and throws a fit if he even thinks you're getting close to saying no."

"By now he should really be more interested in pleasing you," my doctor said softly. "I don't know what we're dealing with. I still don't believe he has autism or Asperger's. There is something along the developmental scale. We need help. Let's start with his speech. That's a key indicator, and he is definitely delayed. It's not only his speech, it's his responsiveness. Let's start with that." By recognizing my fears, he had thrown out a lifeline, a thin cord I could wrap around my son and me, keeping us afloat until the big boat of answers pulled into the harbor.

As scary as it was to be on the trail of "what in the world is wrong with my son," nothing could be worse than another unprovoked attack on a teacher or a friend or, eventually, me. Perpetual optimism about children developing at their own pace could never again be my fallback position. Jack was not developing along any range of normal, and he had increased his reliance on violent behavior whenever hampered in his demand for total acquiescence from the world. I needed to listen to those instincts that I had silenced when they got in the way of ignoring Jack's differences. My steadfast resolve to have a normal son was hurting both of us.

Jack functioned with marginal success when we were alone. I courted solitude, knowing no one else with sense and sanity would consider the pumpkin patch outburst to be merely a severe temper tantrum. It was foolish, even reckless, to separate my son from the outside world because he might be judged and called names along the developmental scale. I just wanted him to carve a pumpkin without an attempted assault with a deadly weapon.

It didn't take me long to find my way to the long road of finding the cure. Recovering from the journey has taken a lifetime.

Chapter Ten

WHEN YOU GET TO THE FORK IN THE ROAD, TAKE IT

Everything in the world of children with special-needs runs on evaluations. Without an evaluation, you needn't show up, because it's the paper, not the child, that lets you in the door. Evaluations detailing your child's unique needs could be the key to extending or deterring emotional, social, and educational progress.

The trick is to know what you're looking for, what you are evaluating, and what you will do with the information once you have it. I knew none of these things when I took my four-year-old son for his first formal evaluation for speech and language, and we both paid a high price for my ignorance.

Jack's total vocabulary that year was fewer than fifty words. My pediatrician had made a successful case for a link between outrageous behavior and his inability to communicate. The local hospital's speech clinic was housed inside cracked plaster walls covered with Sesame Street and Disney posters in an unsuccessful attempt to make the small space seem child-friendly. Child-size chairs, Lincoln Logs, and hundreds of plastic shapes were grouped on a green rug with a chalked circle denoting a boundary.

While I completed paperwork, Jack knocked down a log house and picked up plastic shaped to alternately chew on or throw out of the chalk circle. The speech pathologist entered the room and sat on a child's chair, facing me with a clipboard and giving Jack a speculative glance. Her nametag was partially obscured by the wide collar of her hospital smock, but I think it was Emily or Lilly. She didn't introduce herself.

"What brings you here?" she asked.

I blurted out, "My son isn't speaking. At least, he doesn't say much and isn't very responsive to questions or comments. He is difficult to manage, has a lot of outbursts, and isn't very compliant. He seems to be in his own little world, and we're concerned that his lack of communication is causing some of the behavior problems." Somewhere in the middle of my recital she had put up her hand, and when I wound down from the rising anxiety brought about by her simple questions, she said, "We won't be dealing with any behavior issues today. We will be evaluating speech."

"Okay, good," I said. Only it wasn't good. She wasn't listening. I was nervous, uncertain what was required of me. I didn't want to talk about what was wrong with my son. I wanted to be at some playground with other moms, drinking coffee, gossiping, and telling stories of their child's latest accomplishment.

During most of the time spent with the speech pathologist, Jack worked harder at crawling out of the observation space than at attending to the tasks of evaluation. Completely unresponsive to cajoling and downright defiant at firm instruction, Jack wouldn't look at the cue cards, wouldn't pick up or order the plastic shapes. Within twelve minutes he had rocketed himself into my lap in full meltdown mode. She sighed and told me she couldn't possibly test under these circumstances. "These are the circumstances," I said.

"There is nothing I can do for you now, except to tell you he is very out of sync with other children his age. Without his cooperation, I can't begin to do a detailed evaluation. Unless you can get control of his conduct, he'll never make it in preschool." Our work here was done.

Snaking through the narrow green caverns of the elephantine hospital, Jack sobbed frightened sobs. After following miles of red arrows and then yellow ones, I made for the final set of double doors, pushing the stroller at a gallop pace. Parking the stroller at the hospital doors, I picked up Jack, quieting his anxiety, and guilty that I was the source.

"Bad lady gone?" he asked, nose running and eyes red with tears.

"We're fine now." I bumped the stroller down the steps.

CHAPTER ELEVEN

STUMBLING THROUGH THE LABYRINTH

Years after we ran away from the evil stepmother of speech pathology, her troubling and traumatic assessment would replay inside my head. Her words were like warnings on a tarot card foretelling doom. On the days when our son wound himself up like a tsunami and spun out of control, his swirling rage and absence of emotional boundaries crashed without notice into our world, scrambling our sanity. I could no longer enjoy the calmer times because I was so focused on waiting for the storm to begin again. Our uncertainty over when chaos would strike forced us to the sidelines, ineffective and uncomfortably still. Later I was to learn the virtue of my therapist's advice: "Don't just do something, stand there," a state of being I would have done well to cultivate. I still believed that constant movement was my only antidote to fear of the unknown.

My denial began to extract a heavy toll. Panic attacks, usually involving a ghastly visual of the death and destruction of my family, were beginning to seem authentic, as though I were reliving, not imagining, my fears. Although I always returned to center, there were days when I doubted my strength to keep the car on the road, avoiding the bridge guardrail that seemed to beckon to me, offering me solace in my unhappiness. I didn't think about hurting Jack, although I considered leaving him in a safe place and walking out of his life. Once I caught myself mentally writing a note to a kindly mother superior, including my name and telephone number. Laughing at myself, I knew I was never going to drop him off on the church steps.

"Snap out of it. Stop it or you won't pull yourself back. It's not a game." This was the wisdom of my internal voice, ensuring that sanity still had a place in my world. Most times I listened to this nurturing alter ego. Even with this protective voice and my willingness to concede the power of gallows humor, I was still horrified by my made-up plans for mischief and deceit.

Loving moms do not behave this way.

The speech evaluation was the last one I would ever face on my own. I reluctantly asked Sam to be my teammate. He agreed, although the relationship between us had faltered since our son's disabilities had become the centerpiece of our marriage. Sam was relieved that I was finally looking for help to negotiate the maze of testing that confronted us as we searched for answers. The easy give-and-take that had always characterized our joint response to problem solving was missing.

Because Jack came to us well into our marriage, we had already survived the disruptions and discontent that trouble and sometimes destroy marriage. We had come through the death of parents and the unexpected loss of young friends, dozens of job crises and blistering arguments about rearing a troubled child. During the months since my tirade about his lack of loyalty had pushed him out of my life completely, he distanced himself from me and from his son, less willing to participate in decisions about Jack's behavior. "Whatever you think," became his favored response.

During these periods of our life with Jack, my talent for interpersonal blindness interpreted suggestions from Sam as confirmation of his disapproval of my parenting skills. Long days alone with Jack supported my belief that I could work the magic that would save his life. Jack's safety couldn't be guaranteed unless I was there.

Did I think I would still be tied to my son when he was thirty-five, or fifty? I would be ninety-one years old when Jack turned fifty. How would he live alone? What would bring him to terms with the world around him? If I could avoid it, I didn't think about questions that moved me off center stage. I fought for the starring role in my son's life; impervious to signs that none of my practiced seclusion was actually working. Jack's life was deteriorating, and I wasn't far behind.

Bringing Sam back into the loop of decision-making about his son should not have frightened me. He had never left; he never stopped loving either of us. Tired of constant rejection, he retreated to what he knew best and to where he succeeded: his work as an attorney and the creation of gorgeous perennial beds around our home. Watching him rise at six to be at the office no later than seven, home again by six and then two hours in the garden made me angry and jealous—angry that he receded from me, even though I pushed him away, and jealous because I did not know how to do the same thing. Sam put Jack's perpetual problems on the shelf for a day or even for a week. His capacity for self-care fascinated me. Having pushed Sam away until he stopped trying to help me, I no longer found any protection in being alone, pretending Jack would be fine in a day or two.

Sam never lost track of our son. Supporting Jack in ways I couldn't appreciate, he spent summer days teaching his son to swing a golf club, hit a tennis ball, and dive into the deep end of the pool without alarming the lifeguard. He had a talent for being with Jack, absent the constant observation, never seeking a crystal ball. He was fully aware of his son's disabilities, but I don't think it ever occurred to Sam that it was his job to fix what was wrong. That was my fantasy.

"I want him to be healthier and happier, too. I want that more than anything. I just don't think we're going to find it for him."

My isolationist behavior and Sam's retreat to the only world he could control created a dangerous combination of regret, recrimination, and false independence that would continue to tear at the bonds of love and friendship that filled my life for over twenty years before Jack's arrival. The game of push-Sam-away–pull-Sam-back was reckless. It was just possible that one too many pushes would break the rope, leaving Sam out of my reach. I continued to tempt fate and made a deal with a future I couldn't possibly predict: I'll give more time and attention to our marriage once Jack has settled. It was the light-switch theory of matrimonial responsibility. When life is kinder, I'll focus more on the love I've pledged.

That day of being settled never came, but Sam and I held on. If we had one good day with our son, I was capable of forgetting months of Jack's tantrums and erratic behavior. We ate a meal together, went for a walk, or enjoyed a friend's birthday without Jack creating a dangerous or stressful incident. So desperate to end the nightmare, I saw each of these indicators of normalcy as a new beginning for our family.

Forget that you couldn't string enough happy events together in a month to fill four days.

I pushed ahead with my belief that growth and love would turn the tide. Sam knew I wasn't a fool, but I think he hoped I would stop being seduced by the few twinges of hope I used as ammunition for denying Jack's chaotic history.

As we began the long road to Jack's diagnosis, I was still sure I would single-handedly cure my son. "It's just a phase. He's a late bloomer. He's gifted. He's zippy." I was certain I saw something in him that everyone else was missing. He was beautiful, smart, and funny. I told myself deliverance would follow in the wake of certainty about his disability.

We would find out what was wrong with Jack, and we would fix it.

CHAPTER TWELVE

THE PERIL OF HOPE

To find the cure, Sam and I went on a diagnosis-shopping spree. Fueled by my desire to leave no stone unturned until I had the answer that would free our son and make us whole, allowing us to be a family. Looking for a glittery magical key to unlock the gates to normalcy, I wanted to know what was wrong, but my passion to buy a fix that would make it right was far more urgent.

It seemed there was a new strategy for coping with a new kind of childhood disability emerging every month. We discovered the defiant child, the hurried child, the difficult child, the hyperactive child, the codependent child, and the explosive child. Shopping opportunities included early intervention, biofeedback, learning cues, and smarter parenting tips, and many selections from the burgeoning world of pediatric pharmacology.

Sometimes we feared that the talk, talk, talk was offered to anyone with a dollar and a dream. But after all, when your child is expected to bottom out of preschool, what's the great risk in exploring the community of experts who are using new diagnostic technologies?

These evaluation years lasted from Jack's fifth birthday until just after his ninth. In these roughly four years, we traveled eighteen hundred miles, making stops at five renowned children's hospitals. Jack, Sam, and I met with twenty-four child psychologists, ten pediatric neurologists, seven speech pathologists, eighteen child psychiatrists, and one chiropractor who wanted $100 a visit, four times a month, to realign Jack's "neuro-protection defenses." Then there was the faith healer. She intuited Jack's presence in a Native American tribe, sensing he had been a successful warrior who had come to regret his kill ratio. His soul had migrated to our family so he could exorcise his remorse. Apparently his soul had not chosen wisely. As I said, we didn't miss much.

Sometimes success seemed so close. We could do this. Only we couldn't.

Before we were through shopping, we spent $30,000 that the insurance companies wouldn't reimburse and thirty-five days on the road staying in small motels with swimming pools near the evaluation site, trying to cloak it all in the robe of family time. Throughout this schedule, we cajoled and bribed Jack with promises of playgrounds and new trucks and almost anything that would get him into a room of somber professionals.

Spending our days focused on Jack meant leaving behind reasonable parental boundaries. While on the road, we made daily stops at toy stores. If we needed to produce an even slightly cooperative kid, we gave him the goodies in advance. This pattern would haunt us for years because his expectations developed along the lines of "Give it to me first, and then we'll talk." It is something we still fight against.

We couldn't get his behavior under control so that the professionals could do their job. It turns out Emily or Lilly was right about the circumstances of evaluations: a noncompliant child cannot be accurately diagnosed. Uncertain if they are seeing manipulation, disassociation, or plain crabbiness, we got guesses and requests to bring him back when he could sit for a day of testing. That day never came. The system that investigates children's disabilities has little success in dealing with the child who will not cooperate, even though this unpredictability is at the heart of emotional disability. Jack's fear and loathing of the evaluation process meant that he resisted every effort to quantify and qualify his problems. He made constant demands of his evaluators—toys, food, play time—anything to relieve the focus on his behavior. Early on, one child neurologist told me she got eight minutes of usable data in an hour session. The rest of the time Jack built a fort with her couch cushions. Efforts to distract him from this task brought on the loud screaming that caused me to leave the waiting room and check on progress in her office.

By the end of the journey, I felt truly evil for putting my beautiful son through the rigors of hostile analysis. When he screamed obscenities at the staff, it was hard for me to remember that this behavior was why we were here. He was angry with us for failing to protect him against this assault of probing adults. He was comfortable only when he could set the rules of engagement. He did not want to be pressed to answer questions or to talk about things that stressed or disturbed him.

Walking along the Charles River near Massachusetts General Hospital in Boston after a daylong brutalizing experience at the hospital, Sam and I held on to each other, exhausted by our grief. The day had begun with hearing and vision tests, all benign. Jack participated with good humor, especially in the hearing test that offered a plethora of electronic wonders. The technicians told me the Jack became so proficient with the use of the testing equipment he could probably administrator the next three scheduled exams. He was only half kidding.

The examination for school readiness was a catastrophe. Bored with the absence of equipment and fearful of workbooks and pencils, Jack spent about thirty minutes avoiding the tasks that might have placed him on someone's developmental scale. Then he made a break. Out of the door and up the hallway, the specialist was reduced to chasing him as he careened around corners until he found Sam and me in the waiting room. Exhausted and humiliated by her lack of control over our son (I gave her a break on that, but her supervisors were definitely peeved), "I will not be performing any further testing today," she said. We had waited six months for this appointment and spent $5,500 just to walk through the door.

I didn't blame the hospital then, and I don't now. After all, if Jack could have cooperated, we would have been home making up flash cards and providing appropriate rewards for learning such as ice cream and extra time with public television's *Bill Nye, the Science Guy*. He couldn't do it—any of it. Worse, no one with any credentials in childhood disabilities could tell us what was wrong. We had a list of what wasn't wrong. It wasn't autism, it wasn't Asperger's, it wasn't Tourette's, and it wasn't anything anyone had seen. During the onslaught of indignities concluding our evaluation, we were told, "Give up the idea that Jack is going to Harvard (a fantasy I never harbored) and direct him toward a supported living program. He's at high risk for drug abuse, alcoholism, sexual promiscuity, and suicide. You can't run away from these things by asking more questions. Go home and find a residential school for him. Everyone will be a lot happier. Type A parents with an underachieving kid have a tough time, but you have to accept this."

I managed to make it out of the room without making eye contact with my tormentor.

Jack, mercifully, was with a family friend who accompanied us to provide support. Standing there in the cold afternoon wind and staring down at the hard gray water, we saw members of the Harvard crew team out for a winter workout. Sadness overwhelmed me. I asked Sam to tell me why. "Why did we have to have this child?" Would Sam take me home?

What I wanted most was to go back to life before Jack. I wanted my husband back. I didn't want to live with a father; I didn't want to be a mother. I wanted to be a competent professional person capable of making a good living and producing work that meant something to somebody. Sam told me to stop in the way he had always done when he meant, "I love you." It was the last time we sought an evaluation, preferring to take our troubles and dreams home with us. Nobody had any answers.

Looking back on shopping the system, I often wonder if there is anything that would have prepared us for the price we paid. We didn't find the magic key. Instead we bought soul-crushing inadequacy that deepened our guilt into defeat.

Everything in Jack's life was excruciatingly complicated, but nothing would be harder than the unruly adventure of school. While we were diagnosis shopping and visiting every therapist that had written a book in the last three years, Jack was still expected to show up for school. Every year from preschool through high school brought its own kind of torture. Children with disabilities present challenges for schools. Even if the best interests of the child are a major consideration for the school district, it is never easy. For us, before it was over, it was degrading and nasty, and finally it jeopardized Jack's life.

For many children, the emotional disability diagnosis is a ticket to educational services through a services blueprint called an Individualized Education Program (IEP). Children classified as emotionally disabled may already have a working mental health identification such as obsessive-compulsive disorder (OCD), Asperger's syndrome, conduct disorder, pervasive developmental disorder, or high-functioning autism. Or there may be no reason to slip children into these more formal categories of mental dysfunction. Some children are just restless, anxious, and fearful of sounds, touch, and other ungovernable stimuli in the classroom and at home. In their cases, these classifications may not provide enough information to construct learning and socialization strategies that meet a child's unique needs.

No matter what the diagnosis, no two children are alike. I believe this is why children who can cooperate with the endless guessing game fare better than children like Jack who have no tolerance for being anyone's research. Children are, by definition, unfinished. Personality, tolerance for stress, internal strengths, and weaknesses are not fully fashioned until near adulthood. It turns out that many children do just get better by the time they are eighteen or nineteen years old. For them, nudging their dysfunction along with a few helpful guessing games can't hurt. It may not be important to understand what is wrong, because one day it isn't wrong anymore.

This was not true for Jack.

During early school years, before the school had given him the mantle of emotionally disability, Jack was classified under the dubious label of "Other Health Impaired," a category that proclaimed a problem without providing the clues for solving the puzzle. Some professionals saw him as an educational work in progress; for me it was more like having a thousand jigsaw puzzle pieces in a box without a picture. Without the picture, the trial-and-error method provided our only clues for keeping Jack behind a desk.

Success was measured in weeks, not in school semesters and never in school years. Failure was easier to identify. When Jack stopped getting up in the morning, became abusive at home, and freely talked about how he would have been better off dead, we scurried back to the school for meeting after meeting, trying to find the combination of motivation and discipline that would end the downward cycle.

Many more children escape identification, sometimes succeeding on their own without much help. More often, children who require, but escape, special-needs diagnosis, languish in the back of the classroom until they drop out or get pushed out by an administration impatient with poor behavior and constant absences. These children almost never have parent advocates. For dozens of legitimate reasons, parents cannot or will not be involved with their child's school failure. After sizing up the return on fifteen years of advocacy, I wonder if we might have sheltered ourselves from a lot of pain by giving the school a wide miss. In the early years of Jack's education, we were fortunate to have teachers and administrators who were child-centered professionals welcoming the participation of involved parents. Jack's luck ran out and we watched in anger and confusion as the accessible interested professionals retired and left for more "child-centered jobs" than were available within the local schools.

It's possible that the explosion in the special education lit by the bomb of ADD and ADHD has more to do with the increase in the special-education servicers than any single factor during the last twenty years. Certainly there are children with learning disabilities and social inabilities that psychologists and teachers confidently link to ADD and its three indicators of inattentiveness, "space cadet" personality, and lack of impulse control. Also, parents learned to dread the competition of the high-achieving child who was the darling of America's flagging status in educational excellence. Every child who couldn't sit still now needed a plan. Every kindergartener who didn't already excel in reading required a tutor.

Jack's first IEP was developed before preschool and has been updated every year for the past sixteen years. This exercise continues by law until he is twenty-one, so at eighteen we are closing in on our final three IEPs. Every school district in the country has some similar planning device for children with special needs. When done properly, an IEP can be the right tool to sort out individual needs and strengths, providing a road map to skills and learning.

This is all good news, except that implementing a useful IEP sometimes takes an act of God. Special needs plans are a chart, not a promise. Veterans of the IEP process know that so much else can get in the way of educating any child. School is built on layers of tracking, testing, mainstreaming, self-containment, and small, medium, large, and supersized placement options. Children who learn differently, who need alterative settings, who can't cope with noise, light, varying routine, or bathrooms located around the corner are confronted with a twisted hallway to academics and socialization.

A child who won't attend or participate floats through school for a time. Parents and teachers wait for an inner developmental time clock to tick along until desire and discipline blossom forth from a hidden seed. It helps if the child is malleable and pleasant, harnessing their inner torment or lacking this common ingredient of emotional disability. Then there can be a place to be planted. Many children find their way into this secret garden where limitations and disabilities lose out to the desire to learn. Others never crack the learning code.

We were part of that group.

CHAPTER FOURTEEN

PENISES

Jack's elementary special education aide called me three out of five days by eleven o'clock to come and get my son, because she couldn't handle him anymore. My belief in my own powers to heal soared, while my sense of proportion faded. I should have insisted that the school do its job, not transfer their responsibility to me because I had the flexibility and would come when called.

My son wasn't wanted in school, and I feared for his mental health. He spent hours in a "resource room," a politically correct term for isolation chamber; a place he could be safe but alone, separated from the other children when he was uninterested in traditional learning. I knew that there were reasons for the school's policies. He couldn't leave the classroom at will, wander the halls without purpose, and determine himself what work he would accomplish and what he would ignore.

Jack's IEP called for a full-time aide to shepherd him through the rough parts of elementary school, including staying in his seat and remaining in the classroom. An unenthusiastic middle-aged woman was hired to assist him, one on one, five days a week. Her outward appearance of disinterest I took as a sign of internal patience and tolerance for upheaval. That conclusion was entirely incorrect. Soon, I began to get notes suggesting Jack was difficult, unyielding, and without discipline. I didn't doubt it, but she was the trained teacher skilled at redirecting and encouraging acceptance of limitations. She offered no suggestions and began to call for his removal more frequently. Concerned, I met with administrative staff, wondering if a staff change might make sense. I was counseled to wait, to see if a relationship developed between Jack and his aide.

They weren't wrong. A relationship most certainly developed.

I had spent a particularly difficult week picking up Jack early, but on Friday the call came at nine thirty, barely a half hour after I dropped him at school. An obviously enraged aide was standing in the parking lot waving a sheaf of papers at me before I parked the car. I couldn't see my son. Ignoring her, I moved quickly toward the glass doors in search of Jack.

"Look at these pictures," she followed me and thrust the papers toward my midsection.

"What are they?" I didn't look, but I saw Jack emerge from the double doors and slowly make his way across the parking lot. Extending my hand to him, I was now ready to hear her complaint.

"Pictures I asked your son to work on this morning. They are supposed to be drawings of his family."

I glanced through the pile. All of the people were stick figures. I was drawn as a refreshingly thin person with a wide skirt, no top, and a massive crop of curls fairly representative of my own. Sam was lopsided, one leg much larger than the other, but otherwise about right in proportion to my height. Jack also possessed one large leg and one smaller one. He had placed himself between us in front of what could have been our house.

"So, that's our family. He did what you asked him to do."

"Penises, these are penises." She spat the words at me. "I asked him to correct this two times, and he just made them bigger."

I looked closer, tilted my head, and began to back away from her.

"What are you talking about? He's six and has very little hand coordination. Are you crazy?"

"No, I'm not. Your son needs help."

"Help for what?"

"Sexual aggression. He is expressing it right here on the page. He's old enough to know what he's drawing, and he laughed each time I asked him to draw it properly."

I thought about mentioning that he hadn't given me a penis nor had he bestowed me with breasts. I was androgynous, except for the skirt that could have been a wide fleece because it started under my armpits. I could not imagine what that meant in her book of Freudian dreams.

"I'm not discussing this with you. Please get out of my way." I took Jack's hand and steered him to the car.

"What did I do, Mommy?" Jack asked as I strapped him into the car seat. "She was really mad. I just wanted you to come and get me." I wasn't surprised that he had learned the drill: If I make enough trouble, the school will call my mother. "What did you say to her?" I asked.

"She wouldn't stop yelling, and she gave me a headache. I told her to shut up." Jack rarely saw the harm in speaking

71

without a filter. I forgot to correct his inappropriate conduct, anxious to make it home so I could call the school before my own head exploded.

Jack was removed from her care by the close of the school day. I did take the pictures to my therapist for analysis.

"He gave you nice hair," was all he said.

Relieved by his benign assessment of the childish drawings, I realized that part of the difficulty in dealing with Jack's demons was the danger of accepting unqualified or incorrect diagnoses or evaluation. Once the questioning about "what is wrong with my son" opened the floodgates, every word, every report, every opinion, gained some weight. Sorting it out became a lifelong task.

Jack, no matter how difficult, never revealed an abnormal or unwarranted interest in his or anyone else's sexuality. Still, it was not until high school that I was able to excise this woman's reports from Jack's files. Inaccuracies have a way of following children throughout their school careers and can become a part of permanent records if parents are not extremely vigilant. I often wondered how the uninitiated boss or neighbor would have dealt with this long-ago error if his childish drawings and her vitriolic analysis leaked from his file.

A few months ago, I showed Jack the pictures. "These caused a lot of trouble at one point," I said, handing him the family drawing.

"Why did it cause trouble? I never liked to draw, but I did a nice job with your hair, don't you think?"

"Fabulous," I laughed. "Just fabulous."

CHAPTER FIFTEEN

MY HEAD IS TURNED INSIDE OUT

The speed-pass version of Jack's academic career includes one specialized elementary school for children with autism, two public elementary schools, one middle school, and an emergency residential placement in a psychiatric hospital. High school was rounded out by a boarding school for emotionally disturbed adolescent boys, an alternative high school in another state, and sporadic attendance at his hometown high school. Every step was a nightmare.

Jack's formal education was launched at a carefully selected preschool. We had interviewed preschools with programs for children "who learn differently," or "children who thrive in a creative environment," or finally "children seeking multicultural experiences." We finally had to admit that he wasn't potty trained, but we assured one director that he was adept at changing his own Pull-Ups and would properly dispose of them if they gave him a spot for the trash. That clinched the deal with the multicultural preschool, which charged the highest tuition.

Although the staff welcomed him with lots of attention that first day, Jack was hesitant. He was five years old, nearly a year older than children who surrounded him, but with much less of their school confidence. I sat with him most of the first week until he announced to me, somewhat forcefully, "I don't need a babysitter, I have teachers. Go home." I went.

Early grade teachers were kind to Jack. "His likeability factor is extraordinary," they told us. Through a sunny disposition, a cheerful attitude toward his peers, and a complete lack of interest in school, he achieved a cloak of invisibility, wandering at his own pace with little to irritate or to challenge him. Easily bored, he often found refuge in his assigned coat cubby, crawling inside to sleep. He didn't bother anyone if no one bothered him.

Sam and I confused the feeling of warmth extended toward our son with a conviction that he could make his way through school. Jack treasured belonging, as long as he wasn't asked to produce anything. I began to believe that he would be all right; he was young, and we would support him as he learned in quirky, unusual ways such as saying the alphabet backward while missing three letters every time. Always P, K, and V. By kindergarten he had it down, moving forward and including all the letters. He still prefers saying these twenty-six letters backward and never regrets the absence of P, K, or V.

As more was expected of him as he moved toward first grade, we were encouraged to do schoolwork at home, trying to force Jack's perspective away from free-floating play and provide him with some of the discipline school would require. A short attention span and limited interest in anything he couldn't discover alone at his own pace impeded our progress. I was determined to become a source of inspiration for my educationally challenged son. We would start with a short book.

Settling him on the couch, I asked the question no one had ever gotten him to answer. "Why won't you read the book with me?" I asked.

"My head is turned inside out, and my eyes can only see the back of my nose." He sounded so confident, his logic flawless. By now, most children were reading short books and recognizing dozens of words. Jack's system was different. He would pay attention the first few times he heard a new story, concentrating on the pictures. Over time, he memorized the words, and triggered by the pictures, he always knew if I took a short cut to the end, leaving anything out. But he wouldn't learn to read.

I took personally his refusal to even look at the words on the page. I had dreamed of the intimacy I would create with my child through the world of books. I couldn't accept that reading, so vital to my own life, was beyond my son's interest. I knew he had the intellect. He could read road signs and anything written on the side of an eighteen-wheeler.

Despite his popularity with teachers, Jack's life at school was a daily experience of being out of touch with the talents and growth of other students. I thought I understood the searing need of the outsider to belong. But Jack's isolation from his peers was so much larger than anything I ever had experienced. As he rejected my best efforts to teach him to read, we opened up another way for us to be strangers. I hoped that, like me, he would find solace in faraway places, that friendship with pirates and orphans and princes would protect him from loneliness and fire his dreams. But Jack wasn't like me.

CHAPTER SIXTEEN

MOTHER IS TO TEACHER AS XYLOPHONE IS TO SCHOOL

When the February school break that pays homage to winter sports in the Northeast came along during one of Jack's elementary school years, our family made the impetuous decision to try a happy family activity. School vacations with Jack resulted in greater isolation than those periods where he had some semblance of a school day and random children showed up at a playground for hide-and-seek. During school vacations, other families traveled to the sun or stayed at home for winter sports, perhaps relishing respite from the many structured activities that anchored their days.

In my quest to ignore the evidence that we were different, I decided on a trip to Boston. Sam rolled his eyes but went along, probably more to avoid the difficulties of the six-hour shifts we used to entertain Jack at home during school breaks. So we packed up and went, finding a hotel with an inside pool overlooking the historic harbor and the New England Aquarium. During this trip Jack discovered the cookies and chocolate milk that magically appeared on the costly concierge floor (a reward for last-minute booking), and I discovered a mom with five lovely children.

Fatigued with the weeks of effort to plan a school day that could contain Jack's anxiety when confronted with learning, I was catching on to some unwelcome facts: Jack's internal wiring system rejected formal learning even if movies, art projects, and field trips were the tools.

The Boston trip provided family respite. The hotel pool overlooked ships' masts and the long steely surfaces of freighters waiting for cargo. The harbor seemed dreamlike as the mist rose from the frozen water of the ice-clogged channel leading out to the Atlantic Ocean. I watched as the small streams tried to escape through the mouth of the harbor, only to be frozen as they lost the battle with the colder air around them. My reverie ended at the sound of Jack's voice, very loud, nearing that point of hysteria from which there is little recourse. A tall slender woman moved quickly to side of the pool and spoke quietly to Jack. He swam away, happily beginning a new game with a water noodle she had handed over.

"I'm sorry." I began my pathetically familiar introduction to a new mom. "I wasn't watching and thought he was still sitting on the chair."

"That's okay; he jumped in the water a little too close to my son. He swims very well." Her voice was calm, with a note of friendliness that drew me quickly to the chair next to hers.

"Yes, he loves the water," I said, hoping I was absolved for my negligence.

"My name is Kathy." I introduced myself and asked her to point out her children. When she had counted three daughters and two sons, I laughed, impressed and relieved that here was a woman who might know about the diversity of children.

"School must be interesting. They seem to be close in age."
It never took long to get to my topic of the day.

"Oh, I home school all of them. I started with the first, and
the others just fit right in. I live here in Boston; we just came to
the hotel so we could have an indoor pool."

Answering her questions about where we lived and
introducing her to Sam as he filed past after buying hard-won
aquarium tickets, I wanted to know more about homeschooling.

"We did it because the public schools were pretty bad, and
we wanted to stay in the city. Private school was out of the
question with five kids. I started by joining a home school
association in Boston, and I found out about other families
living near us. We divide up the classes, use other families'
talents (one was a photographer, one worked at the aquarium),
and others give time and supplies."

It sounded idyllic. No schools, no meetings, no teachers to
point out collective faults or cheer us with bright enthusiasm
that couldn't sustain me through the car ride home. Kathy knew
many things about children with learning differences, a term
she preferred to learning disabilities.

"The school's are disabled, not the kids." She laughed, but I
thought I could see in her eyes the shadow of some of my
meetings and the memory of some teacher's forced enthusiasm.
Her children, ages eleven, nine, six, four, and two, were polite
and charming. The older ones were well spoken and welcoming
of Jack.

During the next two days the six children played happily,
meeting at the pool and getting together in one of our rooms
for a movie. They were invited to the concierge floor, where
they politely asked for more cookies and milk while the four
parents talked and drank wine together. It was civilized, and I
felt like a real parent, a feeling I rarely experienced. This family

was a miniarmy and there was always someone prepared to play at Jack's level and within his rigid demands. For a few days I was able to stop apologizing for my child. A notebook full of ideas for homeschooling and connecting with a community we didn't know existed was crammed into my purse, ready ammunition for my new campaign to teach Jack how to learn.

On the drive home I told Sam we either had to adopt four more children or try homeschooling. He went right for the homeschooling.

In my "research is power" approach to this oldest of all education methods, I talked with sincere parents who believed that today's public education offers little actual learning experience for their children. True, some parents were intent on instilling religious or social values. Then there was the family whose tie-dyed headbands didn't prepare me for the family trailer without heat or running water. Their four children listened to Jimi Hendrix, made compost, and constructed building bricks for the back shed, which housed marijuana plants. All useful, no doubt, but not the program I was searching for to awaken Jack's interest in learning. Looking back, I may have missed a step.

I learned everything I could about homeschooling and filed a curriculum with the education department. In the meantime, there were enough "breaks" from school to test our homeschooling protocol. I was still picking him up by noon on most school days. After a snack, I'd pull out the lesson plan and begin with reading a high-interest topic or attempt a trip to the planetarium. I had planned to have him at home by the second grade, hoping he would accomplish some basic social preparedness and a few written and verbal skills.

We didn't get past the first few weeks of Mom as teacher. My vigorous approach to homeschooling was ill conceived at best. His anxiety escalated while his lack of interest in learning was communicated to me in new and ugly ways. Hiding from me at the museums, ripping up classroom materials I prepared, and resorting to hitting and kicking when all else failed, I declared, "School is out" after four long days.

Home provided too many distractions and the space to disappear when he was pressured or anxious. I needed to be in attendance, another difficulty for my child who had by now learned that misbehavior at school usually meant that Mom would be coming to pick him up. That unhealthy codependence began early in our life together. Moms, no matter how well attuned to their child's needs, must separate as their children grow toward independence and self-direction.

When someone asks me today why I didn't home school Jack, I say confidently, "I did." Most of what he learned, he learned when I wasn't trying so hard to teach him, and he was choosing the topic. In our journeys, he and I walked Boston's Freedom Trail a dozen times, saw every borough in New York City, raced through the Smithsonian, and got a private tour of the White House. We traveled the East Coast by train. We planted a garden, took a thousand unfocused pictures, and learned to throw pottery. He memorized the books I read to him. We met Yo Yo Ma, and Jack played one note on his cello while I stood frozen, wondering at the cost of just the instrument's bow. Jack stayed twenty-five minutes at the opera before he declared loudly, "This gives me a headache." He learned to identify all of the instruments in an orchestra, although his current musical taste runs mostly to bass and thumping. He knows the dates of all the recent wars, each space mission, and more about rocket fuel than I could teach him.

The Air and Space museum wasn't busy on a Tuesday morning in mid-February. The guide was patient and respectful of Jack's avid if erratic interest.

He learned about cars and engines at car shows. He fought my presence with rude behavior and disengaged from my lesson plan by outrunning me to the next stop on his agenda.

We didn't succeed where the school had failed. My state-approved homeschooling curriculum lies in a file, untested and incomplete. Jack didn't get a degree or even pass a test.

I did get to be a mom who participated in her son's learning. I didn't join the PTA, didn't make costumes for the school play, and didn't participate in car pool for soccer practice. But I was with my son to see his eyes light up at the unexpected. He can still tell you when America invaded Cambodia, he brings amazing clarity to the topic of bigotry and the dangers of fanaticism at any point on the political spectrum, and he knows what poisonous mushrooms look like at fifty yards. He can't multiply, subtract, or divide, even with the assistance of a calculator.

CHAPTER SEVENTEEN

WANDERING DOWN
THE YELLOW BRICK ROAD

Family travel opportunities had been few and unsuccessful during Jack's early years. There was something in us that couldn't give up on the idea of a family vacation. Experts in child behavior counseled strict routine for Jack, and we listened, building our live around predictable, calming routines that would keep us safe and sane.

Just once, I begged some unknown god of wanderlust, couldn't Jack return from an outing happy with the fullness of what he had seen and done? No matter how unlikely this scenario, I kept packing the bags and giving it another go.

It was blind faith and the seduction of being normal that supported the insanity of taking a highly unpredictable, chaotic, intolerant seven-year-old to *Disneyland*. What were we thinking? And yet, the "happiest place on earth" had a definite allure. This is what families did, and we wanted to be just like other families. We had spent years flailing about in the things we couldn't do, and we were going to have a good time on a family vacation.

California held the additional attraction of being Jack's birthplace. By this time, we had retold the adoption story dozens of times, working it into bedtime stories and silly songs and rhymes that I hoped would let him know how to associate adoption with the positive feelings of acceptance and being loved. Most of these tales and tunes were titled, "Finding Jack When We Needed Him Most." He would ask for a new story or the repetition of one I had already forgotten with the request. "Tell me about going to the 'Specific' Ocean to get me." I would be off on another adventure that predictably ended with Jack, my beautiful baby boy, happily in my arms.

As we got on the plane for Los Angeles, I tried to swallow the memories of nonstop meltdowns that had colored the days preceding the trip. It was clear that even packing for a trip was unsettling to Jack. After I noticed how the presence of the suitcases agitated him, I moved them into a spare room and locked the door. "No going away, Mommy, no going away, I'll hate it," he cried as I folded clothing and placed it in a bag.

Trying to assure him about the plans and the certainty of his own safety only seemed to increase his anxiety. It was then that we mastered the "blindfold" approach to Jack's apprehension.

When it came time to travel to California, he got on board, and we looked just like any other vacationing family. His behavior during flight transfers was actually a notch above the other equally exhausted families making the first leg to Chicago and then on to Los Angeles. Jack was pleased with the miles of hallways that made Sam and me cringe as we sprinted in the direction of connecting flights located in what seemed like a neighboring city. The acres of jungle-gym type railings that fenced off the arrival and departure gates were a special treat, until some safety-conscious flight personnel asked him not to hang upside down.

Jack wasn't at all afraid of flying, and even at age seven had a basic working understanding of the aerodynamics involved in flight, information he improved upon as he grew, impressing pilots who would ask him into the cockpit. There was something to be said about not recognizing the social barriers that keep people from talking to total strangers. Jack was overly willing to share this scientific research with any adult who would listen. His charm and intensity were inviting, and most people listened to him. Some internal radar told him not to share his story with children, and not surprisingly he usually kept away from anyone close to his age.

Cedars-Sinai was our first stop after a daylong flight from New York. We had lunch in the restaurant where Sam and I had dinner with Hannah the night before she went into the hospital. We showed him the mall where we waited through the earthquake and during the two long days before he was cleared to fly home. The site visit didn't go badly, although he was more interested in when the earthquake would come again and whether the mall had a toy store, but that's being seven. I had hoped that even a hazy reference point for how far we had gone to make him a part of our life would reassure and delight him. The next destination was Disneyland.

For many other families, laughter and memories resulted from early rising, and racing at breakneck speed from one end of the park to the other while one family member stood in a two-hour line that might guarantee a trip on Space Mountain. Evenings required complex schemes rivaling rocket science to find food, buy souvenirs, and locate forty-two square inches of space to stand and watch the nightly fireworks. The fireworks were beautiful.

It was August. It was stiflingly hot, overwhelming, and exhausting. It was madness to assume that Jack was facile enough to be pushed and prodded from one location to the next, swept up in a frenzy of rides and attractions. Actually, most mornings the water rides did feel pretty good at temperatures that could induce a coma. Jack was just not flexible enough to be excited about an inner tube doing loop-de-loops at seven in the morning.

He was happiest in the hotel room, watching the same cartoons in the same order he did at home: *Looney Tunes, Scooby-Doo,* and *Pokémon.* He dreaded going out to dinner and became so agitated at the idea of eating with Goofy that he crawled under the bed and secured himself to the bedspring braces with the superhuman strength that sometimes accompanied these fits. We couldn't pull him out without hurting him.

On our second night of the planned weeklong stay, I gave up the battle for dinner in a restaurant and ordered a pizza from room service. Sam did most of the work involved in trying to make this trip successful. However, he was now due a break and left the confining spaces of the room, unable to cope with another night of hours of cartoons to break up the boredom and frustration. When confronted with Jack's intransigence closer to home, we always took turns getting away and taking getting a break.

Sam went to the hotel bar at the bottom of the elevator, cell phone turned on in case I needed help. Jack took his pizza under the bed and asked for the television to be put on the floor where he could see it. I turned out all the lights, opened the curtains, spying on the people in the pool, fifteen stories down. I was suddenly content to be in the air-conditioned quiet, discovering that our hotel room offered a spectacular view of the fireworks being launched on the other side of the parking lot. At the sound of the bright explosions, Jack came out from under the bed, gave me a huge hug, and said, "I love you, Mommy, but I don't like it here."

"I know," I said. "I'm not crazy about it either."

"Mommy?" he asked quietly, "Why did we come here? It's not like home."

"No, it isn't, is it?"

He looked at me curiously, waiting for something from me that would straighten out this mystery of dislocation. "Sometimes people go to new places to try them out, see what else there is going on in the world," I explained, hoping he'd find some reason to stay out from under the bed.

He was clearly disappointed with my reply. He started for his safe spot under the springs, but then lifted his leg up on the high mattress pulling the rest of his body along after him. "I guess so," he agreed without enthusiasm. "I just don't like it. Are we leaving soon?"

"Soon," I said. "Very soon, I promise."

The moon came up, cutting through the silvery smoke of the fireworks finale; people were clearing out of the pool area and heading for their rooms or a late dinner. I soon heard the rhythmic breathing that signaled Jack's sleeping, amazed that he had calmed himself at last. Looking angelic and untroubled, he was blissfully unaware of the madness he had brought into this room.

In an act of spousal radar, Sam quietly opened the door as I moved to the bed. We pulled off Jack's shorts and shirt, slipping on a nightshirt and moving him to the bed farthest from the door. If he got up in the middle of the night and headed for the door, something he did on many nights, he would have to walk past both of us. Usually I slept lightly enough that I heard him if he moved from the bed, or at least by the time he tried the door. Experts had never given us a reason for this nighttime wandering, except that it was based in his anxiety and lack of comprehension over what would happen next. He was worried that he wasn't safe.

Our assurances had not helped to stop the behavior, so we began an offensive campaign that would alert us to his movements, bringing him back to safety when necessary. At home, he usually didn't leave the second floor, contenting himself with sleeping in the bathtub or outside our door. Once or twice he had gotten into the hallway of a hotel before we perfected our system of enclosure. Tonight I wasn't sure that anything would wake me if I got to sleep. I put pillows around the toilet in case he tried to use it in his sleep and fell on the floor, something he had done once or twice.

Pulling the top spread off the neighboring bed, I grabbed some pillows and made a place for Sam and me inside the bay window overlooking the pool and the park. From our bed on the floor, I tracked the moon's trail across the sky until the tears came. Sam's arms came around me, but I couldn't stop shaking, saying over and over, "I can't stand it anymore. Why did we do this?" When sleep remained elusive, I fought to remember what it felt like when I slept through the night, when I was a competent professional and a loving, energetic wife. Rather than soothing me, these thoughts produced scary visions of the overwrought mess of a mother I had become in my efforts to manage the demons attendant to a child with emotional disabilities.

Hours later, startled from sleep by the brilliant California morning sun, I looked back into the room to see Sam, sound asleep with one arm thrown over Jack's body. Maybe I hadn't heard his attempt at nocturnal wandering, and Sam had worked out his own gentle prison to keep Jack on the bed. Moving quietly from the floor, I dressed quickly and left the room, headed for the immense hotel lobby that served all three hotels on the Disneyland grounds.

"We paid for our room for the entire week," I told the desk clerk. "We need to leave, our son isn't well."

"I'm afraid I'll have to see a note from a doctor if you want your money back."

She was not as chirpy as she had been when we checked in.

"Why?" I asked.

"You'd be surprised how many people lie about someone being sick because they decide they want to do something else after they get here," she said, typing into what I could only assume was our Disneyland dossier.

Calling Jack's therapist, I learned he was on vacation, presumably not at Disneyland. I tried my long-time psychiatrist from the lobby phone and got him at his desk. I asked for the required note.

"We can't stay here." I spilled it all out—the terror of Goofy and the claustrophobia involved in spending another expensive night holed up in our hotel room. "We need to get back our money. Please fax something to this number and tell them he's sick."

My doctor came through with some medically acceptable reason to abort this trip to amusement park hell. I called the airlines and was told that switching the tickets to get us home one week early would cost approximately the same amount as actually purchasing the 737 Boeing jet; so we left for the beach that afternoon.

Jack liked the Pacific Ocean, tolerated the San Diego zoo, and was pleased that his next- door neighbor at the new hotel was a girl his age from London who liked to play hide-and-seek. His only complaint for the rest of the quiet, unstructured week was something that would no doubt surprise him today. He was offended that our young British friend didn't wear a bathing suit top. Who would have suspected Jack was a prude? He finally gave her one of his T-shirts, and she agreed to wear it when they went to the pool.

In the years since our first big trip, I have heard from other families that *Disneyland* or *Disney World* were not what they had hoped, and many more who loved it, returning over and over. No one else told me that they had to ask their psychiatrist to engineer an escape. Boys who need solid earth, no surprises, and steady dependency may not do well at *Disney* or on any vacation.

Over the years we have helped Jack to close the gap between his fantasy of traveling and the reality of the stress that it places on him. Today, he enjoys the concept, if not the reality, of travel and is moving toward the belief that he could be comfortable away from home. He has asked for trips to Germany—most likely to try out the 100 mph speed limits on the Autobahn—and considers himself a veteran New York City traveler, even though he rarely ventures from the same itinerary we have used for more than ten years. Traveling thousands of miles to drive at a hundred for twenty minutes would not disturb Jack, but we haven't done it. We do make frequent trips to New York City. We always go to record stores at the newer, sanitized Times Square. He rarely buys anything he couldn't get at home. He will happily make the trek uptown to the Metropolitan Museum of Art and occasionally asks for the Circle Line to Ellis Island and the Statue of Liberty.

CHAPTER SEVENTEEN

CALL ME BRIAN

Seriously limited verbal skills seemed evenly compensated for with great empathy, humor, and curiosity. First on the scene when a friend fell off the slide, first to laugh at the recycled stories about Prince Albert in a can, and insistent on discovering how everything worked, even if it meant taking apart the vacuum or the sink in the school bathroom. He questioned everything.

Much later, Sam and I learned that the constant questioning was actually a language-processing deficit, but during these early years we saw this curiosity in a positive light, telling everyone with a gifted child the story about his hop off the local merry-go-round to crawl underneath for a look at the turning wheel from a vantage point perilously close to the grinding gears. After pulling him to safety with a less than gentle reprimand from the park owner, we couldn't help but envision our own Bill Gates. There seemed to be no limit to our parental fantasies elevating the unique importance of our son's tenacious curiosity.

I wasn't able to understand the flip side of our son's focusing skills until he was nearly twelve years old. By then both Sam and I were frustrated by our inability to get him off topic once an idea or activity grabbed hold. When he was very young, we were still mesmerized by his questions and wanted to share everything we could, especially the story of his birth.

Before I became an adoptive mother, I collected an armful of books to tutor me in telling our story of adoption, to help me to choose the words to involve family and friends who came with questions and mostly unsolicited opinions. Armed with every nuance of adoption and eager to show my confidence as an adoptive parent, I remained in training for the day when Jack would want to know his own story.

Jack's interest in adoption lay dormant until just before his sixth birthday. We were in the car on our way home from school. He began his quest for knowledge with a straightforward demand: "Was I ever in your tummy?" His preschool teacher was pregnant and had explained that her growing bulge was a baby getting ready to be born.

"No, you weren't in my tummy," I answered, gearing up for my long-awaited storytelling fest. I envisioned cups of cocoa and cookies while he sat in my lap at the kitchen table as I parceled out delightful tales of love and commitment.

"We went to California to find you, because we wanted a baby to love." I repeated this well-worn fact, buying time so we could get home, and I could set the scene.

"I already know that." He was offended at my sidestepping the question. "Where was I? Was I in a tummy?"

Okay, there was a detail we had left out. Sam and I were proud of our openness. If we equivocated, we would erode an essential bonding. At the same time, we never admitted the presence of another person. The game was up.

"Yes, you were," I confessed. "The lady in California is called your birth mother. She had you in her tummy."

There, I said it. It was now time to tread the tricky path of a difficult reality: the ultimate rejection by his birth mother and his life as part of our constructed family. Above all, I knew to keep explanations short. On no account would I say, "She was too poor to keep you." Money doesn't make good parents. I had excised this fatal phrase from my vocabulary.

"Why didn't I stay in California with her?" he asked.

"She was too poor to raise you."

Oh, God, how could I? A fuel truck cut me off, trying to grab my front fender. I pretended he didn't hear me and tried one of the lines I had practiced in front of the mirror for years, hoping to get it out this time.

"She loved you, but she wanted you to have a mommy and daddy to take care of you and love you no matter what. So she let you grow in her tummy and asked daddy and me to be your mommy and daddy when you were born."

Taking ample time to mull over this news, Jack turned in his car seat and said with something close to reverence, "Wow, Mom, how did you get her to do that for you? Mrs. Gunderson throws up every day. She feels really yucky."

After this little serving of hero worship, his interest in adoption quickly waned.

"Is this a candy bar day?" Our treat schedule had no basis in fact. When he asked to stop for candy, I countered, "This isn't the day." It worked seven out of ten times.

However welcome the respite, this brief encounter was not the end of questions about his birth.

Two days later he accused us of leaving out more vital information. "Why didn't you tell me I'm Korean?" he bellowed at us at the dinner table.

Why would my blond, blue-eyed child think he's Korean? "Who told you that?" Sam asked, genuinely confused.

"Wei-Wei told me. "

"I thought Wei-Wei was Chinese." Momentarily, I regretted the alternative preschool filled with academic families and parents who had sought international adoptions during the late eighties, when Jack was born.

"Wei-Wei says Emily and Derrick are adopted like me and Korean like me."

"But you don't look like them, do you? Maybe not all adopted children are Korean. What do you think?" Sam asked.

"I think I'm a California Korean. I don't like my name, either. I want to be named Brian. Call me Brian or I won't answer," he announced before he slipped away from the dinner table, anxious for the cartoon we promised when he managed to make it through the school day without a disciplinary write-up.

Finally we had a "child story" we could tell when anyone asked about our son. It was hard to explain life with Jack without letting it slip that he had spent the last evening trashing his room because he couldn't have a friend over to play. We often found it was easier to say; "He's great," offering no details. Our social success status may have increased because of our silence about our child. Parents who fill the evening's conversation with child stories eventually bore everyone. But we were parents, and it was disconcerting never to join the parade of "my child did the most incredible thing." Bragging rights were the reward for all those bad days that no one saw.

Real unaccustomed laughter exploded at the table once Jack was out of the room. Soon I heard the television news ending, and the *Winnie-the-Pooh* theme song began to play.

"There's a new 'Tigger' one, Mom. You like him. Come on," he called as I heard sounds of settling into his comfy spot on the couch.

"Okay, Brian, I'll be right in."

CHAPTER EIGHTEEN

WALLFLOWER

Graduation ceremonies from the sixth grade should have offered an opportunity for happy family times. Jack's grandparents and Sam and I sat through an interminable two-hour program watching every child but Jack receive some kind of an award. Everyone got something, even the girl in pigtails who was recognized for quick thinking during a playground emergency. Jack sat, remarkably, through the entire excruciating event. What promised to be a celebration of some benchmark resulted in an unwelcome opportunity to experience the kind of stinging neglect schools are capable of when forced to deal with a difficult, demanding child.

Our district's mainstreaming policies welcomed Jack's presence among his peers. Once in the classroom, it was clear that the constant negotiation for Jack's attention and cooperation had gotten them down. I still cannot think about that day without seeing my son, realizing he would not be honored in any way, slipping farther down into his folding chair until we had to wake him at the end of the ceremonies. All the while, *I Hope You Dance,* the year's ubiquitous graduation song sung by Lee Ann Womack, was pumped through the public address system until I thought I'd rip out the wires. Ten years later, if I hear the opening chords of this perfectly harmless song I immediately turn the channel in remembrance of my wallflower child.

I was embarrassed that my parents were there to see their grandson sidelined. While I knew he would not be receiving academic honors, I never expected the cruelty of that day's slighting.

I made it into the car before I started to cry. Sitting in the backseat eating his graduation treats, Jack began singing a song he had composed, apparently titled "Mommy Always Cries But I Don't Know Why" to the tune of the *Oscar Meyer* hot dog song.

Sam was angry. "You can't cry every time we go to school. He isn't going to change. What are we going to do? That's what I want to know. You are not helping, and I can't do this," he said with a finality that enraged and saddened me.

"Don't you think I'd like to be back there taking pictures for the memory book? We have no memories. Nothing is worth remembering, because it's all crap!" Tears were a powerful fuel for my worst instincts. Terror found expression in nastiness, and sometimes I couldn't stop once I'd opened my mouth.

"Good one, Mom," came the voice from behind, delighted in catching me breaking a swearing rule. Convinced that I was responsible for his delays, deficits, and disconcerting contentment in his limited world, I felt the familiar claustrophobia that accompanies this indulgent self-loathing. There was no combination of mistakes or bad parenting decisions that added up to Jack's disabilities. I knew this. But I was too far gone to pull back.

Fighting the urge to open the car door and roll to the pavement below, I concentrated on the fantasy of a day when Jack reached deep within his heart and found the magic to dispel his dissonance and disability. He would find his way to something solid, something predictable. He would find his way to me.

"Why couldn't he have Down syndrome or cerebral palsy?" The last words were said out loud. I knew this because Sam looked horrified. Breaking the rules of parenting and sanity in one callous sentence, I had also broken Sam's heart. I could not take in air. Sam widened the distance between us in the small front seat of the car. He wouldn't look at me, but he did check the rearview mirror to make certain that Jack was still in the backseat, something we could never rely upon. Sometimes at a traffic light he would unfasten his seat belt and hop to the pavement. Jack must have sensed the tension, and soon the car was flooded with silence.

"Holy God," I prayed for strength and an end to this ghastly day. The traffic light blinked yellow, and my trance was broken. I pulled in air and exhaled, sobbing. "Who does this? Who thinks like this?" I did.

Back home I still hadn't regained control. Sam and I weren't speaking. It was one of the times that we both found it impossible to remember our common goal of caring for our son and that we were still in love with each other. Isolated in worry and frustration, trust got trounced and communication was blocked by resentment. I pulled my blankets and pillows into the guest room, preparing for the inevitable: When would Sam leave me? When would I leave him? What would happen to Jack? I would take Jack with me; we would be better off alone. I had no proof that this retreat would accomplish anything but more chaos. After all, we were alone most of the time now, and nothing improved, but this didn't dampen my conviction that I could weather my imaginary divorce.

Drifting off to sleep, I visualized the apartment Jack and I would share. A washer and dryer would be nice to have. I planned the furniture, determined to take all my books. Near dawn, laughter won out. I'm not going anywhere. Neither is Sam. I wanted to tell my husband that I had returned to sanity. Back in our bedroom, he was snoring. I left a note, telling him, "I'm sorry, and I love you." Our cat knocked the note to the floor, but Sam read it three days later. He said he loved me, too.

CHAPTER NINETEEN

ASK YOUR DOCTOR WHETHER INSANITY IS RIGHT FOR YOU

Our resolve to fit Jack's square peg into the round black hole of school continued for the next few years. The tragic circumstances that would end his career at public school would be doled out later in sickening spoonfuls of incompetence. For now, we switched our focus to containing his behavior and allowing a few moments of happy family life.

With great reluctance, our family began a series of drug trials, hoping to find the elixir that would narrow the band of chaos that squeezed Jack in its grip. Before it was over, Jack participated in twenty-four drug regimes, sometimes given alone, sometimes in an alarmingly phrased "drug cocktails" that seemed just slightly obscene, considering his age. None of these potent pharmaceuticals had yet been tested on children younger than eighteen.

I can't explain why we continued to explore pharmaceutical options after the first three or four trials ended with no improvement, or worsened his symptoms. Seduced by the claims that balancing serotonin and dopamine could make peace in our son's warring neurology, we'd think, "Just one more try. This one is something totally new. This could help."

The drug trials started as Jack began to free-fall from school. In retrospect, I realize that we were first pushed by teachers to get a prescription for a stimulant. Disorderly, difficult children were rendered cooperative while taking stimulants, and many did do better in school and with friends. As a result, some teachers and school counselors began to practice medicine without a license, insisting that parents seek out stimulant plus anti-depressant medications for the Jacks in their classroom.

After three weeks, his behavior was unchanged, unless you consider that he no longer ate meals or slept through the night and had developed a serious facial tic we were told might be permanent even after we stopped the drug. Three weeks after the end of the stimulant trial, Jack was sleeping, eating, and creating havoc at home and school. The facial spasms took longer to subside, but within a year, he was tic-free and has remained that way, although many children were not as fortunate. In other words, we were back to where we started.

The months Jack spent on stimulants left me confused and troubled by the error-prone doctors, teachers, and other helpers we depended upon for answers. No one had diagnosed ADD or ADHD, and I believed we were willingly led to a drug because we had no other place to go. In time I would understand that this trial and error was the method used with children who didn't fit anywhere but who presented behavioral problems and developmental lags.

One afternoon I found the half-used bottle of the last filled prescription. I called a psychiatrist friend and asked him what would happen if I took an adult dose.

"Why do you want to know?" He laughed.

"I just want to know what a stimulant does. What is all the hype about? Why doesn't it work with our kid?"

"You won't figure that out from taking it; you're not a kid with funny wiring," he answered. "Did you ever take speed, you know, Dexedrine or diet pills in college to stay awake?" His question took me back to the days of "this paper is due in the morning, needs to be twenty-five pages long, and I haven't written a word."

"Yeah, I have, once or twice." I admitted the extent of my abuse of prescription drugs.

"Well, take two tablets and call me in the morning." We laughed at his take on the old physician dismissal, and I hung up, downing the pills.

I watched four ancient episodes of *Bonanza* on cable television, and balanced my checkbook. I stayed inside, fearful of driving, and vacuumed, ironed, and folded towels. These were tasks I typically put off until my family was using their dirty clothes to dry off after showering.

I didn't eat dinner and was back at the television for *Star Trek* reruns until three, when I finally fell asleep.

My psychiatrist friend called me in the morning. "So what did you learn from your experiment?"

"The boring became palatable, and I could lose forty pounds if I'm prepared to sleep only occasionally. I'm a little drowsy but glad to be delightfully unfocused."

"Bingo," he said. "Stimulants hyper focus the patient. For some kids, this seems to help them gather themselves for a day of sitting and other tasks like taking their turn and doing homework. We aren't really sure why. For others, the inner zombie emerges and life evens out, the high and low disappears.

Now you know. Throw out the bottle and no more experiments."

The offensive plastic bottle was already in the trash. I had met the inner zombie who had lived in my son's body while he downed pills. Wasting the day on my stimulant-induced high alert eased my guilt for only one of the 120 days Jack spent sleep-deprived and zoned out in the name of behavior management. I didn't sample any more of Jack's drug trials, but there were more to come, many more.

Treating quirky boys with drugs was the wisdom of the day, and dozens of doctors assured us the prescriptions were safe, nonhabit-forming, and useful. Still, I can only assume it was fear that pushed us through so many drugs trials. What if the next one worked? What if this is his one opportunity? Science had the answers. We still believed it then, but this respect for the expert's opinion took a hit every time we stood by, watching as Jack became hypervigilant, gained forty pounds in two months, fought insomnia, depression, and nausea, and harbored thoughts of suicide—all on medications that we were told would help him to function "normally" in his world.

Giving him the drugs was just the beginning of a drug trial. All family activities had to center around the potential for unknown reactions to these chemicals introduced to his system to calm his fears and open his vistas to include appropriate behavior and learning. Support for this changed behavior included doctor visits every ten to fifteen days, all the while keeping an exact journal of his behaviors as the drug therapy was introduced. My notebook that chronicled a precise diary of behavior was the timepiece structuring my world. Today, two-dozen spiral notebooks now live in my garage. They are filled with every possibly relevant detail from body temperature to the size of his irises in those blue eyes, no longer clear, that had once made me fall in love with my beautiful boy.

Most often, I kept him at home during the first few days of a drug trial, unwilling to trust others with the task of monitoring his temper tantrums, blackening moods, or leaps to euphoria. Jack's increasing volatility drove away all but my most loyal friends. These friends who loved us helped to balance endless school conferences and far too many doctors' appointments and therapy visits. I am still awed by the patience and love it took to include us in a life we could not have experienced without help. There were still so many days that my loneliness overwhelmed me; I was not capable of reaching out to give or receive any sort of comfort, even when I knew it would be there if I asked for it.

During the drug trial phase of our lives, there were certainly people who didn't support us. I still work at depersonalizing each rejection he received. Jack's lack of awareness about so many things meant that he was affected by only the most appalling snubs. There was the time we got a call asking him not to come to a birthday party scheduled for that afternoon. His invitation, the mom explained, was sent by mistake. Jack would be a problem at laser tag. I offered to stay with him so he didn't upset the delicate balance necessary for boys to run wildly, shooting each with light sticks and paintball guns in the dark.

"Better not," she said with what I heard as a vicious assurance for her decision. "He could come for cake and to drop off the gift, if he'd like." With a quick "Bye-bye, now," she was gone.

I lied to Jack and told him the party had to be cancelled. He didn't believe me and wanted to call one of the other boys I knew would be at the party. I piled him in the car for a trip to Toys R Us and bought him a GI Joe. He was thrilled by my largesse. All the way home, I berated myself for using the Band-Aid of material excess to cover up the hurts he would have to cope with sooner or later.

There was soon no escape from my post of constant observer. I disliked the shift from Mom to clinician. Sam took over when I was away, although I had long since stopped traveling for work. I had cobbled together a host of small consulting projects that kept my mind active and ensured that I spent some time with adults. Sam and I frequently saw different manifestations from the same drug. He'd think he was improving, and I saw decline. We learned that both conclusions were possible, hours apart on the same day.

Eventually Jack was declared to be medication resistant, a meaningless distinction that meant the doctors had no more ideas. When I want a nightmare, I can reach back into those days and find fault with our decisions, thinking we may have made the problem worse instead of mitigating it. Sometimes I think we had access to too much information and that my insistence on finding a way out of the daily chaos came with a price he will keep paying. These fears were raised again in sharp relief when my child transitioned so easily to marijuana in his late teens. I'll never know whether the urge to self-medicate came from a history of "Try this, it will help."

"Just a few more years," Sam and I would agree in a rare quiet moment. If we can get him through a few more years, he'll be all right. He'll want things for himself, friends, an education, a healthier lifestyle. Uncertain and scared, I would have believed that the tooth fairy was coming on the next train with the answer to our problems. Nothing had worked in nearly twelve years. I was numb, overstimulated by my constant need to problem-solve, and knew I was staring defeat in the face, no matter how much I pretended. I was dying and looking for salvation.

That's not what happened.

CHAPTER TWENTY

ENTER HERE AND
ABANDON ALL HOPE

The summer before middle school began, a planning meeting with the special-education coordinator ended with this comment: "Middle school is different, and children will either catch up or fall behind."

"The choice is his," she warned us. In a district proud of its policy of mainstreaming children with disabilities, our planning and IEP produced little beyond the decision to place Jack in the resource room, the segregated class structure for "different learners." Jack characterization was more succinct. He called these separate classes the "dummy dump."

Whatever the plan may have been, life skidded out of control six weeks into middle school. On a Tuesday in early October at eleven o'clock, the preferred time for sacking Jack, Sam received a call from the school principal asking him to come immediately to retrieve his son. Met at the door by the principal, the middle school special-education director, the school psychologist, and his teacher – this troop of merrymakers blocked Sam's entrance to the school.

"What's going on?" Sam asked.

"We have a situation here," declared the principal in what Sam reported was his best paramilitary voice.

"Okay, I'm here."

"Your son is threatening to jump out a second-story window." The principal seemed slightly thrilled.

An incident reported in full without ever using Jack's name.

"I doubt it," Sam answered the waiting crowd. "If he's going to jump, what is everybody doing here?"

Sam was finally escorted to the classroom where Jack's behavior had led the staff to believe he was a danger to himself. Sitting on the closed window ledge; Jack was playing with the Game Boy that had been confiscated by his teacher earlier in the day. Unhappy with the loss of his favorite toy, bedlam ensued, and Sam was called to witness the spectacle of a twelve-year-old calmly holding the entire staff at bay.

I got the story that night at home, writing it all down because I couldn't believe what I was being told. Seven adults stood waiting for one overwrought child to act on his threat to jump out of a closed window.

Sam asked Jack to get off the ledge and get his things. Jack complied immediately, unusual but not unexpected given the joy he experienced in the chaos he caused.

"Where's Mom?" he asked. On being told I was in New York City, he nodded and asked if he could go with Sam to his office.

"Sure," Sam said.

Staff had already packed Jack's backpack and emptied his locker. Our son was asked to leave middle school immediately.

That night Sam waited until I was through the door, changed my clothes, and was sitting with a glass of wine before he began to tell me about the "incident."

"Did you hear me?" Sam had that tight around the eyes look that always signaled worry about me.

I couldn't speak. I needed Jack to be in school. When he wasn't in school, he was home with me. "Yes, I heard you. I don't have anything to say. I don't know what to do."

"There's nothing to do. There isn't anything *you can do*." He emphasized the last words, apparently pleading with me to join him somewhere close to the same page or at least in the same book.

I tried to process Jack's "incident," but I drifted off, searching the backyard for a space ship that might have landed while I wasn't watching. I needed to be beamed up, aboard and ready for takeoff. Living in the real world had lost any appeal for me. When I realized that I was thinking none of this would have happened if I had been home, I knew my decline was complete. Did I believe my mothering to be so magical that the whole package of redemption lay just ahead? I needed that spaceship.

"Now what?" I asked the rhetorical question, hoping my husband might have some magic.

"There is no what. We are done here."

"You think we should have him killed?" I got increasingly nasty the more I was pushed into the corner of acceptance.

"You know we can't help him. You know we can't. You've done everything for him. You have no life outside our son. We have no life as a couple. What are you waiting for? Tell me what to do. It isn't what I want; it needs to be what you say. It needs to be what's best for Jack. I don't want him living here. He's going to hurt himself, or more probably you."

Sam had never said this to me quite so directly. He hinted around at his fear about what my much-larger son could do when angered and anxious. I couldn't meet his eyes, and he had known me too long not to seize on my avoidance. "He's already hit you, hasn't he?"

"Sometimes," I answered without any conviction.

"Sometimes he hits you? He hits you sometimes? What does that mean? Is this once a day, twice a week, hourly? Are you crazy that you're not telling me this? What is wrong with you? How can you not involve me in this?"

After the last question Sam took off across the golf course that bordered our backyard. It was almost dark on a foggy fall night. I lost sight of him within a few minutes as he took the trail between the ninety-year-old pines.

I sat there and thought about secrets, the ones I'd kept from him and the ones I never told myself. I was drowning in my determination to love this child forever and ever. This pledge I made to his birth mother had long since lost its meaning. I'm sure we both imagined a different child than the one sitting in his room, stereo up to full volume, unconcerned about another day of chaos overfilling our lives with sadness and pain.

My unflinching attention to Jack's every mood and nuance had caused me to lose track of everything else. I lied to myself about the extent of the violence and discord at home, about my fears for my own safety. Worse, I had lied to Sam and then had expected him to join my fantasy world where Jack was made whole, happy, and independent through the force of my love.

I finished the bottle of wine.

Sam returned after Jack reluctantly went to bed.

"Okay, so when did you start lying to me?" Sam was calm but would not moved by my avoiding the question on the basis that I had everything under control. I lied to keep Jack close to me. I lied to avoid the conversation we were having now. I lied to avoid having to acknowledge the violence that routinely visited our home during the days when Sam was gone. Jack was certainly never going to tell his dad. The fact that I didn't tell probably made me Jack's trusted partner in crime. How often had I mistaken Jack's apparent loving ways as a manipulation to help him keep the secrets we shared? He was the child; I was the adult. From where Sam and I sat that night, I could see how easy it was to believe I was dangerously confused about that fact.

I spoke slowly and carefully, trying to sift out the disappointment I felt in myself and report the facts to the man I loved but believed would never trust me again. I explained how often we yelled at each other, me starting quietly with a request that irritated Jack. He swore and screamed, ugly words that no one had spoken to me—ever. I had become immune to his language. He hurt me, hitting, punching, pushing, and I didn't want anyone to know. I thought it was just me he was hurting.

"So this made it all right; that he was 'just' hurting you?" Sam was quiet, controlling his disbelief.

"I guess it did seem all right, for a while. When he was smaller, I wasn't scared." Jack had been taller than me since he was ten years old. Now I had become afraid that he would push me harder, hard enough to propel me down the steps. I feared his hands, his punches, and mostly the things he would pick up and throw at my retreating body. Chairs, lamps, tables, anything he thought I valued.

"I get that you lied to me. How come this never happens when I'm around?"

"He is afraid of you. You're bigger, and I think he knows that I will put up with it." I needed to confess what I knew to be true. I put up with it. I tolerated being verbally and physically abused by my son.

Sam finally asked me why. Why did I let myself be treated this way? Why did I hide what was happening? "I don't know." I didn't know. I confused love with acceptance of the unacceptable. I distrusted the world that had given us nothing, no answers, no help. I was afraid of losing my son. None of these excuses were answers. They were excuses, and they were all I had.

"We've done everything we can." Sam looked at me and pleaded with me to accept the truth of our son's irresolvable torment. Instead of finding comfort in our thoroughness, this reminder sent me into a mindless, irrational rage every time anyone, including Sam, tried to calm and reassure me with this logic. If we had done everything we could, why wasn't Jack whole?

There were no answers, no prognosis, and no normal child. I had scattered my hopes in too many directions: to doctors, teachers, to the faith healer who urged me to find a quiet place for Jack's soul to heal. Nothing ever came back to me on the wind of my hope.

What I had not done was accept the reality of Jack's life. He was differently wired than his peers. There would always be hundreds of avenues to travel if I wanted to keep moving, dulling pain and reason. Not one of them would lead to a solution; not the drugs trials, not the behavioral modification programs, or the alternative learning plans—nothing would provide more than a moment's respite if we were lucky, or a giant step backward if we were not.

Letting go was another name for drawing a straight line to a lesser life for Jack. He would never achieve independence, meaningful work, or the possibility of lasting love. Was Jack asking for any of these things? Did it necessarily follow that because these milestones were important to me, he had the same dreams?

We sat on the back porch looking out over the golf course as the tops of the pine trees gave themselves up to the night sky; disappearing into the horizon that captures day and relinquishes it each dawn. With the darkness came the specter of the wall I had run into at full speed since I first recognized Jack's differences, the tenderness of the man who loved me, and my own inner voice that pleaded, "Give it up. Move on with grace and gratitude. Make life work." The words sounded fine. I just needed to save myself from the wounded heart that would not let go of my quest for a miracle.

Around dawn we went to bed.

CHAPTER TWENTY-ONE

SUICIDE IS PAINLESS

In the morning after that night on the back porch I started to cry and didn't stop for three days. I didn't sleep or eat or think. I cried. Sam called my psychiatrist on the third hysterical morning and pushed me into the car, taking me to him.

"What do you want to do?" My doctor asked the question quietly while Sam held my hand.

"I want to die."

"That's a choice." He was calm.

"Don't give me that bullshit. It's not a choice. I can't do this anymore. It's all crap. I think I hate my son. I've lost my marriage. I can't do this."

Sam stopped me for a minute. "I'm here, maybe not what we want, but we're still married."

"So it looks like you have a choice to stop doing what is giving you so much pain."

"So we are having Jack killed?" I hated myself again, as I always did when I erupted with these horrific outbursts that imagined harm to my son, harm that would have broken me completely. But it was still a relief to say to the worst, knowing this would be acceptable here. Even Sam laughed. A little.

"You need to stop hurting yourself, and certainly you need to stop letting Jack hurt you." The words weren't clinical, just common sense. But they didn't help.

"I don't know how to stop. I'm obsessed with healing Jack. It's all I think about. Make him well, make him well."

"Your antidepressant medications need to be changed, and I want to see you every other day for a few weeks. You need to promise your husband and me that you won't hurt yourself." My psychiatrist was taking the practical route and insisting that I follow the basic rules of treating severe depression.

I had to consider this promise before making it. I didn't want to promise. I wanted out. Jack's face ran through my thoughts. I remembered that I loved Sam. I still hadn't seen the Arctic Circle. I got out the words and stopped crying sometime during the next few hours.

Driving home Sam spoke only once. "If you lie again about Jack hurting you, I'll send him to a school where he can't get at you." I didn't argue with him. But I was angry. Who was he to threaten me? My doctor's calm face and soothing words also irritated me. Everyone was excessively controlled, while I was losing the defining battle of my life: healing Jack. I didn't know who I was; I didn't feel like a mother, a spouse, a daughter, or a friend. Those were the layers I'd crafted, one on top of the other. But I wasn't anyone. I had left behind my good sense and my grip on reality forgetting the truth about love. Love is not a battleground to be stormed in my manic devotion to healing Jack. More than loving Jack was at stake. I was at stake.

During my week of intensive therapy, I searched the Icelandic Air website for trips to the Arctic Circle. This kept me sane enough to make it to my psychiatrist. After a few days, the doctor told me to choose life, to remember how smart I was, and to accept my son into a heart he was sure was big enough to hold him. One by one, I locked the doors to my craziness and tried to concentrate on living. The short list was Sam. Then there was Jack, my family, friends who would murder me if I took my own life. Finally, that trip to the Arctic Circle would be everything I'd imagined.

CHAPTER TWENTY-TWO

HEARTS IN ARMOR

I was getting healthier, if that meant I was no longer suicidal. My dance around the truth was slowing to a two-step as I once again sorted out the task of distinguishing right from wrong that had guided me through most of my adult life.

Sam watched me for signs of new decline, now certain he should have seen my break with reality coming. Why he taxed himself with the demands of second sight I couldn't say, but I took it in the way he meant it: "I love you, and nothing is worth destroying yourself." That was what he said, but I still was a long way from believing I could have my son and sanity at the same time.

As I climbed back into the world, we were still faced with the ever-present danger of school. Jack needed to be in a school, and we had exhausted the local options.

While Jack was still at home without a school program, misremembering vacations or trips that ended in disaster was a critical underpinning for embarking on my road to normal. I decided to take on another trip. New York City was a known quantity, and Jack reveled in the noise and the frenetic pace. We headed out early for the Metropolitan Museum of Art. The immense neoclassical stone structure was one on my frequent destinations in New York City. With Jack in tow, it was a different museum; his interests revealed texture and novelty in a building I had rambled around for as long as I could remember.

He headed to the arms and armor exhibit in the right corner of the first floor, past the exhibit of Fabergé eggs and solid gold clocks. Again, I marveled at the tiny bodies that sheathed themselves from head to toe with brass and silver. The cost of dying was counted in an older currency during the Crusades, but I couldn't help thinking how all the artistry might have supported life, rather than heralded the extravagance of the kings and queens who sent their men to die in the name of God and property rights. Jack wandered from case to case, finally asking me how he would have covered himself, given the size of the mythic soldiers.

"I don't think anyone back then was over six feet tall. People were much smaller; lived fewer years if the dragons didn't get them."

"There weren't any dragons, Mom."

"Oh," I said, surprised. "What about Puff?"

Ignoring me while letting me see his eyes rolling in disgust, he stood for a long time, staring at an exquisite gold and silver breastplate.

"I could cover my heart with that, but if anybody was any good with his stick, I'd be a goner."

"But your heart would be safe."

"I guess. Let's go see the dead people wrapped in dish towels." He was wandering toward the Egyptian room.

"Mummies, you mean."

"Yes, Mummy, I'm coming."

This exchange carried my hope for days as I rode the crest of his humor, his attentiveness, and a completed conversation.

CHAPTER TWENTY-THREE

FLYING LOW OVER
THE CUCKOO'S NEST

Sam and I had done more than our part to educate Jack. We had spent $30,000 looking for a diagnosis to direct our son's learning. Years were devoted to menacing drug trials. Behavior modification efforts consumed hundreds of hours, and thousands more dollars were spent in counseling services. In those days, the special-education administration hailed us the poster parents for the troubled child; both of us engaged, attending meetings, and thinking creatively about our child.

Healthier now, I resumed the role of chief architect for Jack's educational life. Jack was not allowed back into middle school and had been attending small classes in another building. The entire experience was a nonstarter. After a few weeks of classes, Jack found this new approach to school incomprehensible and lonely. He began to wander the halls, disappear after lunchtime, and visit the nurse's office twice daily.

119

"Jack needs a wake-up call; he needs to be broken down before he can become whole." This hopeful call to psychic renewal came from the nationally known expert I had sought and insisted the district hire to help with Jack's planning. His idea seemed byzantine, and I was soon to find that our expert didn't suffer the interference of moms with questions. This scheme called for Jack to be tutored four hours a day in a locked, windowless, cinderblock cell, smaller than the space allotted to "lifers" in maximum security penitentiaries. A burly young man was hired to stand watch and ensure Jack's isolation from everyone but his teacher.

After two days of hearing reports about the progress of sensory denial and observing Jack's behavior when I picked him up from school, I was told that this was the "wake-up call" prescribed to encourage Jack to fully participate in a school program. I saw a child who was angry and scared, apparently oblivious to the notion that he was "waking up" to anything. But I kept my mouth shut and gave the program time to work.

Six days into the experiment, Jack locked himself inside his bedroom, missing the bus. A few days later he was throwing chairs down the stairs, breaking lamps, tables, and dishes. Twice his father called the local police, who wrestled him to the ground to prevent him from hitting me as I insisted he go to school. The second call was made while I hid inside the downstairs bathroom, seeking refuge from the GI Joe tank Jack repeatedly banged into the door in an effort to get at me.

When the police left, Jack had been hauled from under his bed, and his father drove him to school. I called the carpenter to order a new bathroom door. I don't know what guided me through these assaults on my sanity and my physical safety, except my dubious talent for breaking the day into microscopic pieces, taking each one as a sign that the next millisecond would be better.

My neighbor called to find out if we were all right after she had seen the police car. I told her the house alarm was sending false signals. I called Sam at work hourly, seeking absolution for putting Jack in such a terrible place. He was just as scared as I was; he didn't know how to talk about his fears and I think wondered when he would next be loading me in the car for a trip to the psychiatrist.

The deprivation approach continued to trouble me. The violence at home was growing more frightening each day, but the program consultants seemed unconcerned, as though they had predicted this bump in the road. Sam hovered in the mornings, making certain that Jack was gone before he left for work. Once or twice I called on friends to come if Jack was asked to leave school early. I had promised Sam not to be in the house alone with Jack. Continuing to question the school's uncompromising structure, I feared for my own mental stability while Jack's mental and emotional health was rapidly deteriorating. Intent on following my doctor's advice to stay healthy, I was clawing for solid ground and finding quicksand beneath my dangling feet.

This tough love/grotesque insanity program lasted less than two weeks. I didn't solve the problem of the locked classroom. Jack made it go away.

After a morning of noncompliance at school, Jack was challenged to return to his work. Hostile and unwilling, he left the room for the gym and was taken down to the floor in a split second by the burly man at the door. He kicked and screamed until this man, nominally the adult in this scenario, freed him from restraint.

The call came at lunchtime.

"We had to call the ambulance," the principal's voice came through the line, calm but slightly rushed as though he was missing a lunch date. I was instantly cold, shaking as though I were packed in ice.

"Jack's not hurt, but he has been involved in an altercation so severe that we felt placing him in a hospital was the only choice for his own protection." I could breathe again, but I had no idea what he was saying. Jack was twelve years old. Had he burned down the school, pulled a weapon, or injured another child? I asked these and other questions in the rapid-fire beat that fear brought to my voice.

"No, no," he almost chuckled. "No. Jack kicked a teacher, well, a security guard, and this is how we have chosen to deal with it." I slammed the phone into the cradle and clumsily dialed my husband's work number, punching the wrong numbers over and over.

I couldn't reach Sam at his desk and couldn't summon up the emergency numbers where I might actually find him. I made the trip alone to the psychiatric hospital, bringing clothes, Jack's Game Boy, his long-ago bedtime book, *Goodnight Moon,* and a rage that nearly lifted me off my feet. Sam called just as I got to the hospital doors, telling me he was on his way.

The admissions officer said I could see him briefly, explaining that the hospital could keep him for seventy-two hours on a school's emergency admission.

"Kicking a teacher is a psychiatric emergency? You put him in a hospital for this? Are you kidding?" No response.

"Keep it short. He's upset," he warned.

"I'm sure he is." I forced the words through my lips, incensed that my child's feelings were being explained to me by a hostile stranger.

Stumbling through the quiet halls, all of my senses were absorbed with the white-hot blade of panic carving up my heart. I can't remember what Jack said or did during our brief visit. He wasn't upset. He was just happy to be out of school, counting on the mistaken assumption I was taking him home. Within an hour his father had joined me, looking angry and pushing words at the hospital staff through a clenched jaw that I was sure would break and shatter his face. Hospital administrators gathered around, talking about assessments and workups and new drug trials. I didn't hear a word. That night the nurse called and reported that Jack was highly agitated, and they had to restrain him.

"What did you give him?" I already knew the answer, having read the protocol throughout that long afternoon.

"I gave him Benadryl, to help him sleep."

"Read his chart. He's allergic to it. Jack won't calm down for another three to five hours, especially if he's restrained. If I don't get a call from him in ten minutes telling me he is out of restraints, I'm coming up there to rip your heart out through your throat." I spat out these last words before slamming down the phone.

Sam raised his eyebrows, commenting that the exchange could be considered threatening. Lawyers are a cautious bunch. Eight minutes later, Jack called to say that he told them he was allergic to Benadryl, but they gave it to him anyway. He was released from bed restraints.

Sam and I went back to the hospital the next day armed with educational plans, evaluations, test results, and drug trials.

Sitting across from him at his uncluttered desk, the hospital's clinical director studied the records, fanning out two hundred pages and picking up pieces from the pile to read and nod. The doctor closed the files, asking us, "Why is he here?"

"You tell us," Sam said.

"I think the plan was that this would break him down, and he would then welcome the climb out," I said, sharing the documentation from our school consultant. Glancing through it, this doctor looked hard at both of us.

"This is really insupportable." The doctor sighed. "Your child is not an experiment, and you don't have to be dragged through an emergency inpatient hospitalization for the sake of someone's tough-love policy."

"We know that. We didn't get a vote," Sam said. "Can you do anything for him while he's here?"

"I don't think so. He's too young for our adolescent unit, and he won't cooperate in group therapy. He has a limited grasp of why he is here, and I guess I'm not surprised. This is a psychiatric hospital. Unless he's in crisis or having a psychotic breakdown, he belongs at home with you and in competent therapy."

"Jack has been in therapy since he was six years old. Individual therapy, group therapy, play therapy, art therapy; he's done it all. He's still in therapy, right here at this hospital on an outpatient basis. He's been coming here for more than a year." I gave the report in a monotone. "Do you think Jack is psychotic?" I asked, but I wasn't sure I wanted to know the answer.

"No, but I think his consultant might be." He smiled a nice tired smile. I laughed for the first time in three days. We took Jack home that afternoon. I fired the consultant, who never spoke to me again, despite my repeated calls. If it were in my power, I would have prevented him from ever working with children again. I had to be content with the fact that he would never again be near our son.

"That guy wasn't so bad," Jack said after he had been home for a week.

"Which guy?" I was looking through school catalogs, hoping to see a place called Jack's School.

"The dude that got me locked up." Ah, our school consultant with the tough-love policy.

"What do you think about him?" He had said very little about the whole experience other than his report that "the food at the hospital sucks."

"He was into power. I got that. I hated that place, that school he locked me up in. He told me I needed help, and I wouldn't get it unless I played the game his way."

"What did you think that meant?" Suddenly I had visions of assault and sexual abuse, wondering about "playing the game."

"The same stuff, Mom. Go to school and don't fuck up. I don't know why I can't do it, but I get really nervous, really upset when I get pushed around." Jack was uncharacteristically introspective.

"Well, you tried, and now we'll try something else." I was forcibly upbeat.

"Yeah, I figured you'd send me someplace else. I'd rather just stay at home." Jack looked at me, waiting.

"I know, but that won't help. You're twelve years old, and you need to be in school, a different school, one that you like and that likes you."

"Good luck finding that, Mom." Jack pulled himself out of the chair and clomped up the steps. He slept the rest of the day.

Wounds from the experience of the locked room were deep, shattering each one in our family in a terrifying way. Jack lost his tiny hold on trust and was still viewing me with a spiteful anger that was never seemed far from physical violence. Sam took another step down a road of helplessness that isolated him from everyone. I stopped sharing the truth about my hopes or fears with teachers or anyone in a medical setting. When I was asked anything about Jack, I answered the questions like a good witness and volunteered nothing.

From the moment we busted out of the "biggest dummy dump I've ever been to" (Jack's pronouncement upon leaving the psychiatric hospital), educating Jack became a factory job. I showed up every time I was supposed to be at a school meeting, most often with Sam, sometimes alone. I listened and tried to maintain my slippery hold on rational thought.

School professionals and mental health experts all delighted in confirming, "We have never seen another child like Jack." To the doctors, the schools, and the world of educational evaluation, he was an anomaly. To me, he was my child without a diagnosis, without an approach to learning that would resonate for him.

For the next month he remained at home, usually in his room, usually sleeping. I kept up the search for a school, measuring out each day in negative quotients: I didn't get hit, I didn't scream, I didn't cry. Those were the good days.

CHAPTER TWENTY-FOUR

CHASING THE WIND

Somewhere along our journey with Jack, a mother called me from another state. She was in tears, telling me, "No one who hasn't been there will ever understand what it's like to have a kid you can't control. It's not just about what will happen to my daughter. It's about what will happen to all of us. These people (teachers and doctors) forget that we have to go home with these children. They forget that we are alone for days and days with children they can't manage for an hour."

Amen to that.

I learned a lot from other families who sought my counsel or just wanted a listening ear. Dozens of families have asked me to explain how to encourage (or coerce) their local school district into understanding and responding to emotional disabilities, special needs, and difficult behaviors. My little cottage industry was not a deliberate undertaking. Word of mouth is a powerful weapon for parents with nowhere to turn, and sometimes they turned to me. It may have been the sheer number of assessments and drug trials we weathered with our son that gave my views some credibility.

I told these families that I had made it a priority to get to know my son's teachers and the administrators who employed them. I called them to share information from a recent conference or book. I volunteered in class. And, in the beginning, competent child-centered professionals welcomed our help and promoted our hopes. As with many partnerships, the relationship with my complex and far-flung district soured gradually. Our competent team outgrew the district and the new educational policies demanded more time for testing and less opportunity for teaching. Many talented teachers found jobs at the state education department making policies or in private sector where the pay was often lower but the ability to teach was rewarded. Their replacements were not skilled in special education and understood almost nothing about emotional disability. My attempts at communication and offers to share coffee and lunch were not welcomed. I still believe in exercising care in dealing with the people who are responsible for teaching my child. I saw it work and know that everyone benefited. Then I saw my trust destroyed.

I don't know what motivated our school district's decision to pull away from us, severing their role as collaborator. I know we did what we were asked to do and took full responsibility for our child's problems engaging in school. We prayed for a miracle but we never asked the school to find one. We researched, provided detailed feedback about our family life, often sharing information that exposed the troubled family we had become.

The pattern with the school was always the same. At first, we worked together to design educational plans that would engage Jack. School officials participated enthusiastically—for a while. When it became clear that without a specific understanding of Jack's disability nothing would work for very long, Jack's teachers each took the same course. Fine-tuning or course correction was tried. When Jack still failed to respond, professionals would make another few stabs at finding a way to teach our son. Finally, convinced that another child had learned in the same program, teachers might begin to see Jack as spoiled, undisciplined, or pampered. Then it was time for the school to pull back, to blame Jack and ultimately his parents. Once we reached this stage of strained communication, the only way to get a response from the school was to threaten legal action. So we did, more than once.

As Jack got older, we were routinely counseled by the school to use the family court system, declaring him a person in need of supervision (PINS). My conversation with a long-sitting family court judge confirmed that the family court was not a placement for a child with emotional disabilities unless he had committed a felony. Even his violence at home would not be helped by the services available within the juvenile justice world. In addition, every child therapist with whom I discussed this recommendation was appalled at the notion of turning over to the court system a fragile, anxiety-prone child who had loving parents to care for him. The school was disappointed by our decision, and I will always believe that our choice not to surrender parental rights was the end of any meaningful partnership with our school district.

The school administration began to distance themselves from us after the experience with the locked room. Relationships had turned nasty and finally personal. If I were to advise parents today about working with school districts, I would advise them to move slowly. Parents should consider exercising greater discretion than we did in handing over personal information to teachers. You can't count on confidentiality, and there may come a time that you can no longer anticipate support or cooperation. So choose your words carefully when talking about your troubled child. It is possible to find good partners in good schools, and I believe every family needs that support. There were exceptionally good teachers who never gave up on Jack. I am awed by the resolve of those rare professionals who could be counted upon to rally again and again on Jack's behalf, risking reprimand from district administrators caught up in proving the school's worth, not the student's success. Families like ours with very troubled school-phobic children will have the hardest time sustaining their interest.

Good schools cost taxpayers more money than anyone wants to spend. Bad schools may cost just as much, and certainly arguments about the eventual cost of school failure do not need to appear here. No doubt Jack commanded his share of special education resources. But Sam and I parted ways with the school district when it became clear we had different priorities. Attending to the needs of hundreds of children with special needs may have been a reasonable distraction from the needs of one child who couldn't or wouldn't improve. Unfortunately, I wildly underestimated the triple hinges of ego, power, and bureaucracy that fastened the door and locked us out. In the end it came down to the oldest excuse of them all: the people in charge of educating our son needed to be right. When we questioned that status, Jack's life at school deteriorated, and we lost our hall pass.

There were still a few more years until Jack would be banned from the grounds of the high school and my own name would surface with the descriptor, "that controlling bitch." It turns out some school employees are just as prone to potty mouths as the children they serve.

Shortly after we began looking for a school, my father experienced several ministrokes that let him confused and weakened. The combination of good medical care and his own indomitable will averted the immediate crisis, but I knew my mother would not be able to care for him at home much longer. His sharp mind returned, but he was losing his ability to walk. Suffering as a prisoner of war during World War II, his injured heart first erupted at age twenty-seven. Throughout his life, shrapnel moved randomly through his body, finally claiming an eye. Poor circulation was the medal for frozen feet won after long weeks in a ditch in France. My father was already something of a medical miracle, fooling us every time he went down by rising again.

During this family crisis I made lists, dividing the top of the page into columns: Jack, Father, and Mom, work. I didn't look carefully enough to notice that Sam and I hadn't made the list of "Things I Must Do Today."

Feelers to residential schools had not been promising. Jack had left the psychiatric center in October, and it was almost Christmas. I made a list of all residential placements that might put Jack within the 150-mile radius, the maximum distance I was willing to put between my son and me. Over a two-week period, I covered five hundred miles looking for schools that could handle the mixture of erratic skills and challenging behaviors Jack brought to the table.

A residential program outside of Philadelphia was heavy on autism but prepared for Jack's behavior no matter what the diagnosis. A trusted school professional who had known Jack since pre-school came with me for the interview. This tireless advocate for children never wavered in her love for Jack and her respect for his parents. She was a welcome co-pilot. Jack did fine at the interview, patient with the questioning and reasonably connected to the task of finding a new school. Soon the teachers were making welcoming signs and showing him a room that would be just like his. His eyes started to change, and I saw, just for an instant, that changeling in my backseat driving home from the swimming pool. Without warning, he turned on the teacher and kicked her hard in the ankle.

That was it. They told us they'd think it over, that he was probably just nervous. A nine-hour trip home should have taken us four. We drove through a nor'easter, an ice storm of such frightening intensity that we were slowed to less than twenty miles an hour for nearly a hundred miles. Stumbling into the house, exhausted and discouraged, the answer was waiting on my machine. "Your son is not appropriate for our program. We don't have any suggestions about where he might go. If you can get his violence under control, we will look again at him in a year." The call came through ten minutes after we left the school.

We continued to scour the area for placements close enough to maintain some kind of family life. I spent sleepless night designing scenarios that made home safe, not a "placement" 150 miles away. We could, I reasoned, hire round-the-clock help, tutors, art therapists, play therapists, speech therapists, any kind of therapist that would keep him with me at home. These fantasies led to serious struggles with Sam, who marveled at my tunnel vision and was alarmed at my propensity for punishment. We did not give up on finding a placement for Jack, regardless of the lull in outbursts. Jack had calmed down, now that he was out of school, and I wanted to believe we were done with violence. Maybe after Christmas, we could make another stab at the local school? I was wrong.

The week after I returned from the ill-fated Philadelphia trip, Jack became enraged over something I've since forgotten. He surprised me with a sudden punch to my stomach so forceful that it broke through the scar tissue resulting from an ectopic pregnancy misconceived on the road to adoption. Two days later we accepted an emergency placement at a school for violent boys with emotionally disabilities.

CHAPTER TWENTY-FIVE

MOVING OUT

When Jack went for his initial interview to the residential school, he asked the school director about the policy on runaways. Although not a locked facility, the school relied on three staff for every boy, twenty-four hours a day, seven days a week to ensure scrupulous management and no absences.

"Boys who run away are always found and always returned to school. If you want a locked facility, we will find one for you. I don't think you'd like it. You seem smart enough to make it here. I need a commitment from you that you won't try to leave." The director stopped speaking, waiting for Jack to respond. Jack put out his hand for a high five and that settled that. In his three years at the residential placement, he never tried to leave without permission.

Returning home to pack, Jack was quiet and confused about leaving us. Packing his shirt that said: "I'm Awake, What More Do You Want?" He took his telescope, and his World War II weapons directory. On the last trip to his bedroom he took his grandfather's Purple Heart packed inside the leather box that smelled like the basement of the house where I was married. He asked me if I would keep his favorite toothbrush. I forced out a smile, determined to be calming, and said, "Sure, you'll need it soon." Jack's toothbrush was in the bottom of my purse for three years as a talisman for his return.

Leaving Jack at the school dorm was one of the most difficult things I have ever done. We smiled, Sam held my hand, and I went back two or three times for "one more hug." Jack looked uncertain, putting on a brave face because there were other people around. He didn't cry. Standing with the staff, he shuffled to the dorm door, kicking the dirt. I thought he might turn around, so I kept my smile firmly in place while getting back into the car. When he took one last look, I was grinning at him, giving him my silly wave that usually embarrassed him. That day he just smiled at me, and then he was gone.

The following week I drove my parents to Florida to keep myself busy and get them away from the winter. My father's health was now stable, and I was pretty confident they could handle a month on their own. After settling them into their rented house, I made my way to the airport for the flight home to life without Jack's presence. Weather problems and missed connections resulted in a thirteen-hour return trip. I filled the time with worrying and writing a letter to Jack. I don't know if he ever read it, but I mailed it from Philadelphia, one of my many stops on the return journey north. Here's what it said.

Dear Jack,

This week I drove your grandparents to Florida, hoping they will stay for the winter. You know that Grandpa is sick and is failing faster now. Soon he will go "gently into that good night." He didn't write these words, but he always told me he believed death would

135

*be like going to sleep; that once sleeping he would
dream of himself as a younger, healthier man. I
believe he will dream about you as well. Grandpa and
Grandma love you very much.*

*Tonight I am on a 737 plane flying home. This trip
was supposed to take four hours with one stop, but
I've been to three airports and started my day over
twelve hours ago. If you were with me, you'd tell me to
"Chill!" and you would be right.*

*Just two weeks ago Daddy and I left you at
school, away from home and us. I know you can't
understand our decision and that you are feeling
scared and maybe angry. Daddy and I are also
scared, but we will all be fine. Sometimes families
can't live together, and this is our time to be away
from each other so that we can come together again
and live happily as a family.*

*You are still part of our family, and we won't
forget you just because you are not home.*

*I thought you might want to know what it is like
being your mom. When I first saw you the day you
were born, I had no idea what it was going to mean to
be a parent. Like many moms, I thought more about
having a baby, actually about getting a baby, than
about parenting a child. You don't like it when I tell
you that you were beautiful, but you were and still are.
A force of nature that knows nothing about sadness or
regret designed your face.*

*Before leaving for school, you said to me, "You
just want to get rid of me, because I'm so much
trouble."*

*Let me tell you the truth about that. I was not
prepared for the tasks and losses of loving a child with
your problems. Sometimes I felt that we were
strangers, especially when you were angry and trying
to hurt yourself or me. I had grown so comfortable*

136

with my baby bunny-boy and the long days we spent laughing together and learning how to love each other. When your dad returned from work, he would ask me what I did all day. Often I told him, "I laughed and then I watched Jack's face."

I spent those early months falling in love with you. It's something moms and dads do. I hope you'll find that out for yourself with your own son or daughter, but not too soon!

Later, as we began to understand that you weren't growing like the children around you, I fought against your different development, unwilling to see that anything was wrong that couldn't be cured with a kiss and a nap.

When you are older you will learn about the different ways your problems have been categorized and how we used medicines, therapy, and learning strategies to find the answers we thought would help you. Your dad was your best ally in the struggle to understand your problems, and I was often not very nice to him for the order and calm he tried to bring to both of us. I saw his acceptance of your differences as a betrayal. Daddy says to me: "Jack is our son. We will always love him, but he isn't who you want him to be."

Daddy loves you very much, and someday I hope you will be able to thank him for loving us without needing the assurances for the future that I needed. I needed normal, and I believed I could make that happen for you and me. I glued you to my hip and held on, daring the world to separate us. But we were lucky. Your kind of chaos and uncertainty needs two parents, and you have them.

Soon you will be thirteen years old. You will grow in the quirky ways that move you through the world of your own choosing, continuing to absorb what interests you and reject what doesn't suit you. Once in a while, when you are very angry you say to me, "You're not my real mother. I don't have to do what you say."

Do you remember how I answer you?

"If you know anyone who is willing to do this homework (or whatever the fight was about), bring her on." It hurt me when you reminded me that I wasn't your "real" mother. But, I know that giving birth doesn't make a mother. If I had given birth to you, would I have had a better road map? When you were very young, I was disappointed that you didn't want to read because reading was the solace of my childhood and the inspiration for my adult life. Would you have inherited my obsessive reading gene? I am fascinated by everything in our world, especially by its people. I want to understand who gets to define grace, why some people make the rules and other people with good sense are simply ignored. If I were to choose a life of crime, I'd steal valuable art. My clumsiness if not my moral core will no doubt result in staying the course of a writer. I love the part of the earth made up of water and think that God may be in the ocean or on the wind that drives the currents. As your father's biological son, would you still be tall, crowned with black hair that turns silver over time. You might have been an overachiever driven by the potent mix of our joint determination to succeed. Your dad is a loner; he talks to flowers and he takes joy in the wicked fun of watching people behave badly. He's a news junkie and can be brutally frank when unmasking pretense. His sarcasm stings and has wounded me more than once.

Your father and I bring shortcomings and imperfections to a world that pretends to have neither.

*We have made poor decisions, we have caused one
another pain and each betrayed the other, breaking
love and trust. We have treated each other with
kindness and with a lack of grace, with love and with
disrespect. We have loved each other, lost each other,
and found our way back again. We have been lucky.*

*Our lives are not the blueprint for your happiness.
We haven't understood your choice to live in chaos. I
think you squander too many chances, and I worry
that payment will come due for your extravagance.
You wear out your world; expecting people will
continue to come around again and again. They
won't, you know. People grow tired of offering
chances and will leave you behind. In offering you
help and love, people offer a piece of their soul. Don't
reject it. And remember that families don't just
happen; people who need each other and are willing
to be needed in return must make them. Families love
each other forever and ever.*

*The pilot has asked us to put up our tray tables, so I
think I'm finally landing. Remember that I love you.
You and Dad are my family. We have a lot to fix, but we
are still together. At the end of the day, the only thing
that matters is that we keep showing up, keep trying.*

*Tonight's sky is filled with stars so much larger
than seen on earth. At 35,000 feet I believe they were
put there by a higher power; God, ancient spirits of
the sun, or the great mandala; that wheel of life
pictured on the inside of your world history book.*

*I don't know how love happens. Hearts are
fragile. All we can do is love one another. You'll be
back from school soon, stronger and happier. But
when you decide to leave home for good, you can take
everything in your room, even your Great-Grandpa's
rifle, the one with the barrel filled with cement. You*

won't have to pack-up the love. Just look up at the
stars. I'll be there.
Love,
Mom

During the time Jack was gone, we saw him every twenty-five days. After a few months, he was able to come home for weekend visits. He went year-round to school, something critical to his management and progress. While with the staff, Jack came to know things about himself and his attitudes about his world, probably for the first time in his life. He wasn't "broken down and built back up" but was confronted daily with a realistic picture of his behavior.

Initially, Jack was not interested in relearning social skills or developing academic habits. He lived to goad the staff into sending him home. Through patience and the demands of group living, Jack finally managed a delicate grasp of the consequences of his own actions. Settling into a quiet rhythm of school, counseling, recreation, and community service, he did his homework, made his breakfast, and was fastidious about the single room he earned next to the exit door. He said he felt like he was somebody.

A young teacher, whose approval was important to him, restrained Jack after a fight with another student. In the three years he was there, he was never again restrained. Nonviolence was a code of conduct, and he saw something in it that we had never been able to illustrate for him: compliance works. Good behavior opens doors to movies, pizza, hiking, skiing, and cliff diving, a form of recreational insanity I watched just once. He got up every day to show up for something. It was often a struggle for him, but it was a huge step forward. I tried to seize hope from his progress without questioning why he wouldn't recognize the same incentive and rewards available to him at home.

CHAPTER TWENTY-SIX

THE CALL

Without the stilled memories of happy family baby pictures that are constantly moved across my desk, making space for the debris of writing, I might forget the promise of earlier days entirely. It would be impossible to envision those times when I hoped to float above the vortex of Jack's whirling behavior. His placement at residential school should have brought me some respite.

After Jack moved to school, many people urged Sam and me to travel: return to London, where we met, take a walking trip through Costa Rica, plan weekend getaways to reconnect with life and each other. Oddly, I didn't feel free. I didn't think I could go to the bathroom without my cell phone. Sam was equally disconcerted by the idea that we would now go out and build a life in the absence of our son. During the eight weeks we agreed not to see or talk to him while he settled in, I painted mental pictures of his abandonment, his chagrin at more tough-love discipline, his confusion over where we were and what we were doing without him.

The time arrived for our first conversation with Jack after the two-month embargo. Jack filled us in on the vital statistics as we sat in our family room on two extensions. I mined for a wide vein of detail as I listened to his strong voice, realizing that we rarely talked on the phone.

"I don't know why I'm here with these drug addicts and perverts." It wasn't a question, just a statement of the facts, as he wanted us to know them.

"Is that who's there, addicts and perverts?" I asked, not entirely convinced he wasn't on to something. Maybe I should bring him home. "Stop it," I told myself.

He continued with disarming carelessness. "Yeah, this place is whacked out. There's lots of 'safe time.' You know where we 'channel our energies to do well.'" He lowered his voice to report this last information in his funny psychiatrist riff. The filter of my anxiety quieted any laughter I might have had for this "we are all safe here" imitation of his over-evaluated life. This child had spent more time with therapists than classmates. Did he have any defenses in the world of troubled-children school?

"What do you talk about?" his dad asked. I didn't think we'd learn much, but I blessed Sam for changing the thrust of the conversation.

"Just all kinds of crap: respect, education, finding my inner guide." Jack laughed at the end, pulling me into his world that disregards attempts at rehabilitation of any kind.

"We get reports from the school, Jack. They tell us you are doing pretty well. You've made a good adjustment. Tell us one good thing," his dad persisted, refusing the temptation to feel bad for him.

"I cleaned the trash out of the river. There's a place to sanitize the metal and plastic. My art teacher helped me build a sculpture—she calls it a sculpture. It's a B-52 bomber, but she doesn't know anything about warplanes and shit. Still, it's pretty cool. When the paint is dry, she said she'd hang it in her shop."

"Where's her shop?" I wanted details.

"Some place downtown. You could find it, because this place is so tiny. I'm more of a city boy. Not enough going on here for me. It's really a dump. When are you coming?" He was cycling back into negative speak, his favored method of communication.

"I don't know. We have to get permission from the school," I said, still digesting when he had become a city boy, living all his life in a tiny suburb.

"You can't come to see your own son? Now that's messed up, Mom. Aren't you the boss of me anymore?" This last referred to an ongoing discussion about the degree of power I had over his life. He had long ago decided my right to authority was questionable at best.

"We're still the bosses of you. When you went to school, your dad and I also agreed to follow the rules, so they tell us when we come."

"Mom?" he asked.

"We're here. You're not coming home right now." I sounded firm, just like a boss.

"I know that." He drew the sentence out as though he was explaining himself to a slow-witted listener.

"I just mean you should come for a day. There's a movie theater and Taco Bell. It's pretty lame. Also I need Tide."

"You need Tide? Why?"

"The detergent here is crappy; it makes your sheets scratchy. I want what you use at home. So come to see me. I gotta go. Come soon." He cut the connection.

143

Chapter Twenty-Seven

Remember Love

About six months after Jack was installed at school, Sam and I did take a trip, not to London, but to the Carolinas. We had been there with Jack several times. We should have tried Nepal or Paris, but I was busy not letting go of Jack.

Sam wasn't fooled by my unwillingness to venture into territory we had not explored as a family. I suspected he was annoyed that I couldn't take advantage of this time when Jack was safe and gone, when we could have planned our own adventure. He knew I needed to be someplace where I could envision our son. He may have not have known that I was disconcerted at the prospect of being alone with my husband. Years of putting Jack first left little time for anything approaching date night.

The vacation was a shaky first step toward renewing our couple status. Now that we were alone, it felt more like an awkward third date, enough information to be intrigued but no idea if this relationship would take off. Most afternoons I sat on the beach, reading or writing in a journal. By unspoken agreement, we sought out time alone as much as time together.

We were beyond tired and felt pushed by well-meaning friends and therapists who urged us to ignite the magic of marriage. Not sure if I would know ecstasy if I saw it walking toward me, I preferred to delay the search and try to get some exercise and some good wine.

A noise near my beach chair distracted me. Shading my eyes, I looked up from my book to see a kite flyer standing between the ocean and me.

"My God, he has sexy knees," I thought. Flexing, relaxing, and flexing, the patella's slide across the tendons and ligaments was mesmerizing. Positioned in a low-slung beach chair, the beach heat and steady wind urged me on in a frank appraisal. My gaze raked higher, flicking up over respectably taut stomach muscles. Next came well-formed hands wrapped tightly around a large, bulky Pro-winder. This giant kite steering device tethered a silk scarlet bird, guiding it skyward when the wind trapped its wings. Knees now at rest, muscles articulated in a graceful curve that flowed downward to ankles just visible through a heavy veil of sand.

I was hooked.

I pulled myself out of my chair and sauntered over. Aiming for a slight je ne sais quoi, I asked softly, "You fly your kite here often?"

"Shit, could you grab that line? I need a heavier tail." The kite took a downward dive, landing bird face first in shallow water. I held on tight while he detached string and wire to free the beast. "What did you say?" Sam had obviously not read the article on rediscovering your spouse that I had left open on the coffee table back at the house.

"I didn't say anything." I struggled with the kite paraphernalia that was three times larger than the bag it came out of. Soon he would say, "You have to fold the kite the way it was folded before," but for now I tackled it my way, pushing and stuffing.

"Nothing," I repeated. "You had to be there."

"I am here," he reminded me, giving me that pained look that crinkled up the corner of both eyes. Sam was still talking.

"You have to fold it the way it was folded before." There, he said it.

"Right, I know," I said. "Are we finished here? I want to get something to eat." He took the bag, began to refold the stuffed fabric, and asked how I could possibly be hungry. "We ate breakfast three hours ago."

That was just mean. I thought we had settled the "I can be hungry when you're not hungry" conundrum. "So what if we did? I can still be hungry."

"You can also be cranky," he assured me.

Communication may be the foundation for intimacy, but active denial and selective hearing were also mainstays in my approach to marital longevity. Kite folded, we made our way up the dozens of steps cut into the steep dunes. Turning back for a look at the sea, my eyes filled with tears, overwhelmed by the beauty of the remote spot and the certainty that the knees were coming with me.

Sam and I have been married forever and ever. No one observing our first meeting would have bet on us as keepers. A bus carrying students from Milan to Paris through the middle of an August night was the setting for lightning to strike. Bridge-playing maniacs had disturbed his sleep. He asked for the seat next to mine. Because my head was in it, I would have thought the answer was obvious.

"Fine." I sat up with an unwelcoming grunt.

"My name's Harry," he announced. My face was now twisted against the icy window that leaked frozen air throughout the eternal ride through the Alps.

"I hate that name," I complained, my breath visible in the sinking temperatures.

"What name do you like?" He seemed interested, not offended.

"Maybe you could be Sam, or Caleb, or even Bruce, but not Harry."

"Sam," he said. "I'll be Sam." He had my attention. A man who is willing to change his name for a bus seat qualified for a second look in my dating pool. It was dark. His hair had that purple sheen that glows like ebony in the sunlight. Lifting my head, I shifted in my seat and began to slip to the floor. His arm shot out to prevent my fall. Suddenly he pulled back and crossed his legs to make a platform I could push against and sit upright. The awkward struggle had left him in disarray, his khaki shorts riding up past his knees. My God, he had sexy knees.

After so many decades, time loses its sharp, sequential edges. It's hard to remember when we bought the log cabin or how often we've been to Florida. The full-spectrum rainbow, slashing the Galway sky with a violet to crystal white color band, is still a point of pure bliss. Words to capture the birth of our son materialize only briefly, manifesting in a joy that isn't spoken. Deaths of people dear to us left wounds that are the same yet different for each of us; in the way we are the same yet different. Missteps and misdeeds struggle for traction against the strength of our joint history.

Now, as we rode our bikes back to the beach house, I thought about our anniversary celebration earlier that month.

We ate dinner at a new, expensive restaurant and drank too much wine on a weeknight, putting aside the duties of parenting and jobs. He handed me a fat envelope after dessert. Inside was a brochure for a trip to Iceland.

"You want to stand on the Arctic Circle and see the Northern Lights," he remembered. "Now is the time."

The magic was still there, right inside the two of us. It is sometimes harder to find, more difficult to sustain. As Jack's parents, this trip was an opportunity to sleep as much as possible more than the romantic holiday friends may have imagined. I still found a miracle. There on the wide beach I found the frayed ends of the thread that has held us together through the years of challenge and heartbreak.

When Jack is out of control, it is easy to lose the strands of my life as Sam's spouse. Its purpose, its joys were tangled in the web of becoming a mother to a child with serious disabilities. Commitments to family, friends, and work also fell into a distant second, third, and fourth place to Jack's immediate and insatiable needs to be protected, nurtured, pushed, and pulled back again.

Long ago, when the terror of Jack's troubles haunted my days and nights, Sam made a decision that he shared with me: "We need to come first, and if the choice needs to be made, Jack will be the one to drop out of the equation."

I knew he was right and even felt sure of the unconditional love that defined our life together. But when it came close to calling the question on Jack's place in our world, I pushed to go another day, to continue walking the fragile ground that still made us a family. Sam always agreed in the end, but there were days when I knew if I had shown any readiness, we would have found a way out of the constancy of Jack's upheaval, a way back to life with two instead of three.

Sam loves Jack. He doesn't need defending for his commitment to parenting his troubled son. When he could have given up the struggle to be supportive of our son, who wanted no part of him, he fought to save him, to spare me, and helped me to find the path to family I kept insisting was waiting for us. Sam insisted on respect, family values, and a zero-tolerance policy for abusive behavior. I would like to say we were totally in sync on these solid ideals of good parenting and successful family life. But we were seldom together in assessing the danger. I looked for signs of hope even when the cupboard was bare, and Sam stayed the course, believing nothing was worth sacrificing our marriage. When I wanted to be angry with my spouse, I would silently accuse him of treacherous behavior: Who gives up on their child, no matter the pain and chaos? I felt forced to choose—son over husband. Sam never asked me to do that. His world is set up differently than mine. He thrives on order, dependability, and discipline. We had none of these gifts with Jack. Sam thought we couldn't live without them. I couldn't live without either Jack or Sam.

Needing that never-discovered diagnosis for a road map, a certainty of disability to help me sort through what was acceptable, if irritating behavior; I spent most of Jack's childhood believing I was the difference between his success and failure. If he refused to attend school, I wanted to design a new and better approach to teach him. When Jack's doggedness about having his own way made it impossible for him to keep friends, I became his constant companion, believing I would model successful conduct, and he would mimic me.

This force of my will was grandiose, improbable, and the only way I knew to mother this child. I never stopped searching. Failed attempts at school, appalling language, and outright physical abuse were not enough to warn me off of the someday treasure of Jack. One friend described my resolve as "optimism on steroids." She laughed but cautioned me, "Steroids are dangerous. Be careful you don't lose reality in all this Mary Poppins brought to life."

It took me years to understand the strain I had placed on my marriage with my constant cheerleading. I wasn't paying attention to my husband. He wanted a commitment from me that we were more important when Jack's behavior threatened our safety and our sanity. I danced around what I would do if the "him or me" question got called, looking for a day when all would be well. Although I have wondered how I rejected the evidence of Jack's decline with such unwavering blindness, I've never doubted that we both wanted our marriage to survive.

When our marriage was periodically threatened, we talked to therapists and purchased a dozen books about marriage and living with disabilities. Some experts told us to set aside date night filled with sparkling repartee about anything but our child. Other mental health counselors suggested joint hobbies that involved us in each other's passion. Others went just for the passion, promoting sex as the answer.

Any of these solutions might have worked, depending on the problems identified in the handy quiz sections of these "become your own counselors" books, but I remained skeptical. I never met a moment of sexual bliss that could erase the pain and doubt of a child whose fuse could be lit with the scrape of the chair leg against the wooden floor, flaring into flames that consumed the oxygen from our universe. Nothing, not joint interests, or money, or exotic travel, can fix broken hearts invested in a child who can't be healed.

But we kept trying, staying together against the odds. When I considered the naive twenty-three-year-old bride, waltzing down the aisle while more focused on the flight time for the plane to London than on committing my lifetime to the virtual stranger standing beside me, it is still miraculous to me. Longevity is endurance counted in numerical currency. The passage of time can have meaning or be a mean reminder of how far off track we wandered.

Well aware that the divorce rate among couples raising children with disabilities hovers at nearly twice that experienced by couples differently stressed, I wasn't unaware of the risks I ran in rattling the cage that holds my priorities. I knew I wouldn't make it on my own. Not only would I be unable to master the skills needed to raise Jack alone, I did not want a life without Sam. Praying to the unspecified spirit who protects marriage I have asked with the selfishness that love allows, "If there is a God, let me keep what my heart treasures, give me strength before my heart breaks." So far, somebody has been listening.

Chapter Twenty-Eight

Does Anyone Know
Where I Went?

After Jack was born, the decision about who would go to work and who would stay at home was made largely along practical lines. Sam's law practice required presence and staff. Most people were under the impression that I could write anywhere. I thought so, too, until I tried to do it. For a while I was able to arrange my work schedule around Jack's frequent school absences. Sometimes I fit in the work between the hours of midnight and 4:00 A.M. because I couldn't settle him or myself for a moment's clear thinking.

When Jack went away to school, I went back to work writing and providing governmental relations support for a small not-for-profit agency. Truth be told, I started work again because I missed the office atmosphere, the replay of the nighttime soaps, the welcoming break on the way upstairs to my fifteenth cup of coffee. I missed having people around me; their presence kept my thoughts and actions under control. Rows of open doorways and colleagues in search of a laugh or a confidence kept my personal emotional breakdowns at bay.

Before Jack left for residential school, my life had no pattern except the one he chose each day: Would he go to school? Would the school want him gone before noon? While he was at boarding school I was not as tethered to his outbursts and incompatibility with the day's planned events, although I got the occasional call from the teacher who couldn't corral his interest or the nurse confused by Jack's constant visits to her office. The school dealt with Jack's foul language and even worse temper without involving us. To me, that was a miracle.

On school breaks, Jack continued his uneasy relationship with friends, often needing to be picked up an hour after he was dropped off. Who could blame any frustrated mom who wanted my son out of her child's life? These families had their own issues, and although I would have given my right arm to walk in their shoes, how could I be so confident it would have been an easier path? That was part of my blindness through the years: not appreciating that normal is a wide highway, and nobody who parents a child gets a free pass.

Sam assured me that I spent too much time worrying about Jack while he was safe and gone, reminding me I could now be more in charge of my own schedule. I didn't feel like I was in charge of anything. I was too used to jumping when the telephone rang, to rushing to retrieve Jack when I sensed he was about to unwind. The school was qualified to resolve the day's catastrophe and even to offer some balance and sanity. But I rarely let go, feeling I might need to make the ninety-mile trip at any moment. I don't know if it was worry, fear, or jealousy that someone else could handle my son that kept me hyper-vigilant.

But, I began to let go of Jack and looked toward the task of making a stronger life. I knew I could continue to love Jack without the daily drama of his life at home. I began to believe I could love myself more if I was brave enough to step out of the shadow of his disability. We were doing the best thing possible for our son by placing him at a school that would be able to meet his needs. Even so, I never really gave up the battle to see this decision as an act of love, not abandonment. I needed to accept that having a life of my own did not mean I was turning my back on my son.

There was always one place I found solid ground and acceptance. A few enlightened and loving women friends handed me the keys to sanity through the simple act of sharing their children with me. During these lonely years when Jack was healthier away from home, these women made certain that I was a central part of birthdays, Christmas, bas mitzvahs, proms, and graduations. A wise inner voice told me to grab hold. This gift has also filled me with gratitude for friendship that splintered the glass wall of my isolation and rescued me with a call to come and be part of family life.

I volunteered for the Girl Scouts, shouted, "Encore!" at school plays, and cheered at soccer. These children and their families gave me what I did not have at home: a child's dreams for the future and a role in helping them to come true. Through their generosity of spirit, I discovered that no family is perfect; no one sails through the rough channels of childhood without getting wet.

Some of my cherished "kids," now young adults, remain in my life. They embrace my love, sometimes ask my advice, and bring me great joy. I'm a mom by acclamation. I celebrate my good fortune. It is a gift that gives me the strength to reaffirm my love for the zippy child who calls me Mom.

CHAPTER TWENTY-NINE

MY FATHER, HIS FRIEND

My father died just after Jack began his second year at boarding school. He loved his grandfather with a depth I had never experienced in the company of this brilliant but remote man. When I was the child, he was often away from home, traveling the country weekly and yanking the family through eleven moves that furthered his career and our quality of life.

Moving is emotional motion for a child, no matter how lovely the new house, how gracious the neighborhood, how reasonable the opportunity. Nothing but fear of rejection propelled my brother and me through the unfamiliar doors to another school where we rummaged out a place to belong until the call came again.

Through it all, we had learned to dazzle with our footwork, nimble and ready to take our seat. We both became quick studies, mapping out the trends and rules of each new locale within weeks. When my new seventh-grade teacher made me stand to "tell the class a little something about myself" in a school near Washington, DC, I was no longer terrified of the routine.

With a confidence more from habit than belief in myself, I stood up and said, "Hi, I have a dog and a brother, but I like the dog more. I hate math, but I'm good at history and writing. We're only going to live here for a few months, so if you want to be friends, let me know. I won't take up a lot of your time."

My self-characterization got a laugh, so I used versions of it through three more moves, until we were done and stayed in one place so we could graduate from one high school. I can only imagine my mother's constant worry and my father's bold belief in the future that must have supported this company man's self-assurance. For the vagabond brother and sister, life was full of unwelcome surprises. Yet we mastered it. Now when I stand to speak in front of twenty or two thousand people, the butterflies are there, but they are in check. When I had the chance, I dug roots and stayed where I was planted for thirty-eight years.

As my father aged he found a slower pace, became a homebody with patience he couldn't tap during the years we lived in the same house. My father could sit with Jack for hours while Jack sawed through wooden sticks and used a pound of nails and two gallons of glue to create what? Grandpa always gave the concoction a name of "aviary condominium" to "firehouse loft for firefighters sleeping outside for reasons only they would know." The two communicated without incident, with love and trust, making me wonder about the impossible pattern of Jack's behavior, predictably concluding that something I had done to my son brought out the ugly side. Jack rarely showed temper or impatience with his grandpa. He tuned in to this older man's pace and vulnerabilities, disabilities from war injuries, and heart attacks that made him largely immobile for the last year of his life.

When I finally forced the question of a nursing home on my mother, who could no longer cope after years of caregiving, Jack was angry with me. "You lock up everybody when they don't do what you say." He certainly had a point. From his perspective, it was "Don't mess with Mom, or she'll have you sent away."

Jack was on a weekend break from school, still angry about the nursing home. He called me "the jailer" and worked himself into a full-blown meltdown over his decreased access to his grandpa. Finally, my own guilt kicked in, and I packed a small bottle of scotch, two rocks glasses, and headed for the nursing home. Stealing ice from the hall machine, I arrived at my father's room at eight o'clock, after visiting hours. The darkening September night was quiet, bedtime at the home. Father was dressed, sitting in a vinyl issue chair, watching playoffs on the television Sam had installed that morning in time for the World Series. Other than this new addition to the décor, the only other personal touch to this stark, discouraging space was a small throw, red and stitched with the words, *My Grandpa Loves Me.*

"I brought scotch," I said to him. The alcohol was off limits for a man with serious congestive heart failure. Since longevity was no longer in the running, a few minutes of stolen satisfaction seemed like a good second place prize.

"Make us a drink before they catch you." He was clear on the rules. He had lost the use of his body, not his mind, making the imprisonment even more terrifying.

Over the next two hours we sometimes watched the game but mostly sipped small drinks and talked.

He was sad, and remarkably, he told me so. "Not from being here, I know why I'm here. I miss your mother, but it's okay.

I'm glad you got me the private room. There are a lot of screamers here. The people here are nut cases. That's the worst. That and the cheerful nurses who really do ask, "How are we?"

I was nervous when I was alone with my father. We didn't have a great history, and it was too late to think about history. There was just enough scotch for a third drink for each of us. I eyed the oxygen mask hanging on the wall above the bed, jumping when the nurse filled the doorway with her great good humor. Damned if she didn't say, "This is nice. How are we?" She must have smelled the scotch. Maybe it was the look on my face, but something made her withdraw.

"Are you all right?"

Startled by my father's question, I spilled scotch on the tiled floor.

"Hey, don't waste that." He laughed and started to cough, in a frightening and familiar routine. Signaling me with his outstretched hand, he assured me, "I'm not going to die until the scotch is gone."

He wouldn't.

"Why don't you tell me why you came out here tonight, not that I don't appreciate the refreshments. You don't like baseball."

"Yeah, I do. I like baseball." I couldn't remember if I liked baseball or not. I needed to talk and couldn't find a place to start.

"I wanted to thank you for being a good grandfather. Jack is crazy about you. Thanks for loving him and not asking a lot of questions." Was that what I wanted to say?

He considered me through a long stare. "He's a good kid. He'll be all right. You need to take tighter control." He stopped talking.

I didn't want to go down the tighter control, more discipline, teach him respect road. It was a dead-end path to walk with parents, family, and "I want to be helpful" friends.

"You don't think I was a very good dad, do you?"

"No, no, you were okay, you were good." I slumped into the chair, hearing how the faint praise damned.

"I was good? Good. On that note, I can die happy." He was smiling at me, but I couldn't stop the sudden release of sobs that had wanted out since Jack had called me the jailer. I was grateful he didn't try to say something to comfort me.

"We never connected on anything. You were there for us, for our family, but never for me. I danced and danced, and you never noticed me. I went to the college you went to, I majored in journalism. I read every book you read." This all came out on a long breath.

"What did you want me to do while you were doing everything I did?"

"I wanted you to say I was a good daughter, that I was talented, pretty. I wanted to be the best daughter."

"You're my only daughter." He stated this fact quietly.

"So, I win by default?"

"Why do you call me Father? Why don't you call me Dad?" The question veered into a wide turn away from my emotional outburst pleading for confirmation of smart and pretty.

"Because I always have. I don't know why."

"Yes, you do. You distanced yourself from me. Father is formal, Dad doesn't need so much, and it just is. I'm your dad. You didn't need to live my life. I never asked you to. Telling you things you should have known already would have wasted your time and mine. I told you what I thought would help, what nobody else would tell you. I don't say I was right. That's just what I did."

It was a long speech for him, even in healthier days when he didn't need oxygen to slow his heart. He wasn't finished. "You're a woman now. I haven't liked all of what you've done. You should have worked harder. You have an agile and competent brain, but you lack discipline. You must know how smart you are. You're too serious about your politics, too severe in your judgment of people. You think I'm prejudiced, but I think you're intolerant. You have great intellect, but you're held back by your expectations. You want much more than anyone ever gets."

More sentences strung together than I had ever heard in a lifetime. He wasn't done.

"You're a good mother. Jack is a good boy. I wish you'd had kids sooner. But you were busy. You were working at important jobs; making more money than I thought was possible for someone so young. I thought you should have had five kids. You're full of love, but you don't know how to let go and let life happen."

He had never said I was good at anything. I was mute, shaken by the words of praise.

"You've got to be brave, or life passes you by. Take yourself less seriously and work harder at love. I love your son; maybe I can, now that I'm dying. You gave me a grandson. You did a good job with that, too. Do you think that's enough 'good for you' for the night?"

As I gathered up the glasses, I looked at the alcohol level in the small bottle. Just a drink left. I left the bottle, telling him he had more time; there was still scotch.

"Good, that's good to know. By the way, Jack calls me grandpa, not grandfather. I'm not a goddamn Heidi movie."

That time I did laugh, out loud.

"That reminds me. You have a good laugh, not a lady sissy laugh. I always liked listening for your laugh."

"I don't think I can stand any more praise. I'm glad Jack has you for his grandpa. Sometimes I'm a little jealous. You two have your own little world."

"Yes, we do," he said without apology, his voice strong and certain.

I needed to go.

I didn't kiss him; we were unaccustomed to comfortable affection. I put my hand on his arm and told him to hide the stash, and I started toward the door. Just as I reached the handle, I heard him speak, very softly.

"I love you." I didn't turn around, afraid he'd actually said, "Good night."

Walking through the double doors to the parking lot, I breathed in the nighttime air, finally got it out. "I love you too, Dad," I said, as far away from his hearing as I was from him.

Five weeks later when Jack was home for a holiday break, my father became very frail. Jack spent most of one day sitting with his grandpa, pushing the wheelchair around the halls and outside when the sun was warm. He stayed for dinner and then didn't want to come home when I came to get him. Finally untangling himself from the cords that made the bed go up and down, he folded himself into my father's lap, trying to fit his six-foot frame into the tiny chair. My father ruffled his hair, kissed him a dozen times, and told him to limit his video games to an hour a day.

"Ninety minutes, because I don't get any time at school," Jack negotiated.

"You're not supposed to play games at school. That's why they call it school, not a video game place."

"Okay, for you I'll do it."

"Do it for yourself. You're the one who needs the discipline." He was starting in on another generation.

Jack listened, kissed my father's head, and jumped from his lap to the top of the door, hanging there, impossibly long and slender. When I left, I stooped to kiss my father, too. He didn't seem surprised. On our way to the car, Jack asked why I was crying.

"I'm just happy you had a good day," I said.

"Then why don't you smile? You're a little strange," he summed it up for us.

"I know. Get in the car."

The call telling me that my father was dead came at four o'clock the next morning. Sam told me to go, that I could do this by myself. He would stay home in case Jack woke up. He would tell him.

It was just dawn when I arrived at the nursing home. The nurse, my father's doctor, and the coroner were all there. His door was shut, and a blue ribbon hung on the handle. Qualified to act for my mother, I got through the paperwork but never went into his room. I thought my mother should be there first. At least that's what I told myself.

I woke her a few hours later and took her to her husband for the last time. She sat with him, and I paced the hall.

"We have a lot to do today," she said, emerging from his room. "Say your good-byes."

I went to my father, clutching a sheet of graph paper in my hand. Jack had made a map of a video game, trying to explain the strategy for his uninitiated grandpa. I brought it with me to give to my father, sure that he could channel from beyond to track Jack's computer time. Placing it in his pajama pocket, I said, "You were a good dad. I love you. I always loved you."

Then I shut the door.

My father's death was Jack's first experience with loss. He held himself together, proud of the relationship he had with his grandpa and pleased that my father's love for him was so well understood by our family and friends. I gave the eulogy at the funeral, always getting the speaking parts at family events. Jack told me it was a good speech. In the middle of death, praise from everywhere.

When his grandpa was buried at Saratoga National Cemetery honoring his World War II sacrifice, Jack helped my mother take the flag and saluted the honor guard. Jack asked for three extra days of vacation and got it. He spent most of the extra time with my mother, talking about his grandpa. He didn't turn on his computer for another month. Jack took his grandpa's well-worn 1962 chrome and red plush desk chair after I cleaned out his grandpa's home office. Even when offered more modern chairs, Jack has never relinquished this relic of his grandpa's working life. It's just a guess, but I think his grandpa would accept that most of the time Jack is sitting in the chair, the computer is on, and the keys are flying. Jack often talks about his grandpa's presence in his life. If he could unlock a calmer space filled with discipline, I believe he would try as hard as I did to win the respect and love of my father, his grandpa. The secret he may yet learn is that he has already won this precious commodity. Perhaps he will come to appreciate, sooner than I did, that love and respect were always there, always free for the taking.

CHAPTER THIRTY

RECONNECTING

Our first visit to Jack after he left for school should have been exciting. Life at home had developed a rhythm all its own without him, even though we often fixated on the mountains that could be seen from behind our house. Jack was in school just over the ridge, yet a world away from us. We talked about him every day, and within a few months, memory began to alter. The life we remembered with Jack was not the life we had had with him. In our memory bubble, we were all happier, calmer, and without the need to send him away to school.

Weekly discussions with the school administration set the time for reconnecting with his family. Although I experienced the need to see him as a sharp pain near my solar plexus, I was hesitant about making this first trip after months of telephone calls. Nervous, afraid of being manipulated, and unsure how to be a visitor in our son's life, I didn't want to lose my tenuous grip on the beginning of a different life where I was not always unhappy. I had made some progress letting go of Jack's every mood, every nuanced problem, and feared that I'd lose what I had fought so hard to gain.

The reunion was a success, or so the school reported to me the following week. Jack seemed unimpressed that we were there but wasn't openly hostile. He hugged me quickly and shook hands with his dad. Staff and a few friends were introduced, and we briefly toured his dorm. His room was immaculate. We had lunch, saw a movie, and shopped. We probably spent too much money buying him "stuff he really needed": the longed-for Tide, a yellow vacuum cleaner so he wouldn't have to wait for the battered dorm version, comic books, and car magazines. Seven or eight boxes of Little Debbie treats rounded out the cache. Everything was purchased at the Wal-Mart, the only real store in town. It was one of the most normal days we had ever spent together. I asked very few questions, and he didn't have much to say to me.

He took some pride in showing us the back roads of the rural community that had become his home. We stopped at what looked like an artist supply store, drawn to a steel structure hanging in the window. It was his B-52 bomber, and it really was brilliant. Strong lines formed by recycled soda cans and gallon milk jugs. A synthetic oilcan was forged to form the heavy body. The propellers were each a slice of aluminum, cut and bent for speed. The sign in the window said *Face of War* by Local Student.

We had him back at school at the appointed time. I got a long hug and a kiss. He hugged his dad. A young staff member came out to the drive, put an arm across his shoulder, and stood with him while we pulled away. Jack waved, picked up a basketball, and began a one-on-one game that I watched from the rearview mirror until they both disappeared from sight.

The following Monday, I called the art store and asked about *Face of War*, explaining I was Jack's mom.

"Well," this shop owner and environmentalist artist explained, "we're not supposed to talk about the students, but since you already know his name, I guess it's okay."

"I'll tell you this much. One of my fancy Boston art collectors wants to buy it. I told him it's not for sale. He offered me $400 for the plane. Said it shows '...rare imagination and eclectic form.' I don't know what that means. He talks like that. I just know your son could be good, really good, if he worked at it. I can't get him to do much, but Jack seemed to like this piece." Finally she wound down, giving me a chance to make my request.

"Can I buy it?" I was certain she would want me to have it.

"It's not for sale. It's part of my permanent collection at the request of the artist." She laughed. "Tell your son you want it, and then I'll get it to you."

I asked Jack about it several days later. He was silent at first, and then said, "It's not for sale. Sorry, Mom, I want it here."

I never acquired the *Face of War*, although I often hinted at wanting it. It may still be hanging in the permanent collection.

Jack's life continued an unhurried transformation at school for another two years before he made a reasonably successful transfer to a nearby alternative high school that was also out-of-state. The school was purpose driven to divert boys from violence, moving them toward self-discovery and learning. Once into the routine, rules relaxed as he earned and held the trust of both adults and peers. Consequences for violent behavior became internalized so that he was able to draw on the experience before drawing new blood. Of all the changes he made, his skill and affection for conversation was the one that surprised me most.

Almost three years to day he had left, he returned home. I wanted him to stay at the alternative high school. He was doing well. There were only sixteen other students, including two girls. He was done with being away and, playing into my need to have him back, he finally won the day.

I would soon understand that the skills Jack learned from his stay at school don't travel well. At home, he missed the intensity of the staff support and the individual attention. He rarely resorted to physical violence, although his language deteriorated to foul and then to astonishingly obscene. For a time, I tried to convince myself that all fifteen-year-old boys spoke this way, and many of them did. But he used crude language without a filter. He would tell me to fuck off with as much ease as we would verbally attack a teacher.

Seeking relief from my scatological son I asked my psychiatrist for an explanation. He told me that when one difficult behavior is conquered (in this case Jack's physical abuse), another less difficult but still troubling behavior might emerge. We had that in spades. I hoped that while he was at school, some inner resource would be tapped, and Jack would learn the value of education and discover more tolerance for the uncertainty of his emotional dysfunction.

Not only did that not happen, in many ways, Jack was the same boy who left us three years before. This does not mean I thought the school failed or that the struggle wasn't worth the cost. Jack had a thicker skin. He no longer expected the world to accept him as is. He showed a resignation about his life that both pleased and troubled me. He understood that he needed to participate in life if he wanted anything out of it. He was also sadder, quieter. Jack kept his own counsel, perhaps a reaction to group living. He was less impulsive, less volatile, and happier to be alone.

Although all of these qualities were potential building blocks for high school and the future, I was uneasy and couldn't talk about it sensibly. I felt something was different, sadder, but I couldn't name it or decide whether it was a bellwether for pain or progress. Sam thought I needed time to get to know our son again. It was as though we had delivered to school a lively, difficult young boy and three years later, gotten back a more mature, slightly introspective teenager who was a stranger to me and not very interested in knowing me. Finally, I decided to view the school as a success and focus on the steps to come. There had been too much invested in his leaving to interpret failure at his return. I needed to get to know him again.

Because Jack's school program was year round, he returned home at the end of his tenth-grade year. At home, his class was in the middle of the eleventh grade. After we gave him a week to settle in to his room and to inventory the friends he remembered, he was asked to meet with the school district administration.

We were pleased that so many people remembered him and had enough courage to remember the good parts. We were still working with a team of school professionals devoted to Jack's best interests, and that meant they worked hard to assemble a workable transition schedule. He attended classes regularly for a few months. He was doing schoolwork, getting passing report cards for the first time in his life, and keeping his outbursts under some control. He had very few friends, because even those who could accept his behavior had moved on to activities he couldn't master, like team sports or an acceptance of the importance of academics.

His language continued to deteriorate. Sam and I both tried to keep this annoyance in perspective. He wasn't hitting and was going to school. We reasoned that we needed to let the obscenity-laced conversation slide. School professionals at that time in his life understood his emotional disability and were prepared to deal with his language, finding it far preferable to his violence.

For five months, everyone, including Jack, worked to make a miracle happen. Even so, Jack could not be in a mainstream school. He could succeed in a lifestyle that included school, but it must also include twenty-four-hour staffing, clear consequences, and professionals used to dealing with boys who skid out of control without warning or provocation. He was unable to pick up the vestiges of teenage life. He had no place in school, no friends available after a three-year absence, and no prospects for the future that held any interest other than getting a driver's license and finding a girlfriend.

Chapter Thirty-One

Who Knew He Could Parallel Park?

Glass sidelights wrap around the front door to our home. Standing just out of sight of the see-through panels, I watch as ginger-color sunrays collapse across the front yard in the fading afternoon light. Leaping off the front porch, Jack's long strides take him to the driver's side of the car in a few steps. Unaware that he is being observed, he raises one fist into the air and shouts, "Free at last, thank God I'm free at last" before he opens the door and climbs behind the wheel. The engine fires, and soon the taillights trace the curve and wind on up the driveway, stopping briefly for a slow left turn and then disappearing into the traffic.

Today Jack passed his driver's test. Certificate stuffed deep into the pocket of his tattered cargo pants, he was alone at the wheel and tethered to me only by the cell phone he carries and sometimes turns on.

Feeling foolish standing in the darkened foyer, I move down the hall to the kitchen, grab the results of the road test, and scan the sheet, quickly grasping its simple grading system: A for intersection skills and signaling, B for passing and lane changes, D for observation skills in traffic, and an A for three-point turns and parallel parking. During the thirteen-month challenge to teach Jack to drive, he never attempted the task of parallel parking, even though I told him it was a necessary humiliation in the quest for a license. What is a three-point turn? Presumably I've been doing them for years or at least was never cited for failure to complete one. Whatever it may be, Jack excels in its execution.

The D for observation was disconcerting but not surprising. Jack lives in a limited-vision world of the here-and-now, but it did seem insupportable that some weighted scoring system didn't trigger a failing grade for anyone who is a high achiever with the turn signal but has no idea where he is or what he's turning into.

When we arrived at the testing site earlier that day, I pulled the DMV employee aside and offered him fifty dollars to flunk Jack. My whispered confidence and the cash offering surprised him. Jumping back slightly, he gave me a cautionary look. "Usually," he explained, "this bribery thing works the other way around. You know, nervous Mom really wants her kid to succeed so she asks me to go easy on the parallel parking."

Signaling to Jack to get in the car, he smiled, saying, "He'll be fine, don't worry. You want to ride along?"

"No, I want the ground to open up and swallow me, " I thought, but skulked off in silence to a nearby tree to wait. "We'll be back in ten minutes," said the instructor, still eyeing me warily as they pulled from the curb, signal flashing appropriately.

This was our second visit to the motor vehicle test site. Six weeks ago, the money for failure scheme hadn't come up. I had limited hope of success with this approach anyway, and Sam had warned me that it was probably illegal. "How can it be illegal to ask them to fail him?" My own misgiving that he might actually pass propelled my appalling lack of concern about swapping personal rights for an uneasy peace with the terror of a teenage driver. Sam told me to stop it and breathe.

This rite of passage is never a guarantee for boys driven more by impulse than insight, and Jack's expectation that a driver's license was packaged with his sixteenth birthday was first met with extreme parental resistance.

As the magic date neared, an unsteady confidence grew within me, sparking a metamorphosis that surprised me and astonished family members and friends. I became almost defiant that he would get a driver's license and become a safe driver. My conversion was rooted in memories of a conversation with the mom of one of Jack's classmates during the three years we were looking for autism as the answer to Jack's behavior. It wasn't. But my friend was a wellspring of comfort. The mother of five children, her youngest diagnosed with autism, she had something I didn't have: normal children who responded to normal parenting practices. Worried about her son, she told me how anxious she was for him to pass his driving test. "No young adult is ever really independent if they don't learn to drive," she said with experience that couldn't be disputed. Those words stayed with me and ten years later moved me from "absolutely not" to "absolutely."

So we jumped in, insisting on six months of driver's education, sixty hours of road time, and waiting until his seventeenth birthday for the road test. For all of Jack's facility with the computer, it took him months to schedule the test, even though this event was the calendar by which all things were planned: "After I get my license, I will…" was the warning shot for dozens of future events. The deal was that he needed to make the arrangements and prepare for the test on his own. Paperwork, detailing the road test and what he needed to bring to the test site, sat on his night table for weeks.

That first attempt to take the road test was a disaster. Knowing how it would end (the requirements were clearly printed on the paperwork), I braced for the fallout. Arriving without the proof that he had completed driver's education, the instructor dismissed him quickly and told him to come back when he was prepared. Jack had not read any of the instructions. With his usual mixture of bravado and blindness, he had done it his way, resisting guidance, assuring me he knew what he was doing.

I took no joy in the outcome. On the way home, Jack got out of the car at a stoplight, slamming the door with such force that the plastic panel popped off the dashboard. Stilled to silence behind the wheel, I felt like a traitor for not handing him the keys to the test. Fostering self-reliance as he took on this major responsibility was the right decision, but that didn't help. Rolling up behind him after he'd covered about three blocks on foot, I spoke quietly. "Get in the car. It's getting dark."

During the next six weeks he stopped driving for a while and then asked for help to reschedule the test. With only minimal assistance, he picked a date that would require early dismissal from school. Locating the driver's education certificate, he put it in an envelope, putting it in the drawer next to his bed. On the day of the exam, he was ready, checking and rechecking for the papers and permit.

I imagine the instructor never told him about my treachery. Whatever he might have heard in that car, he emerged with an unfamiliar taste in his mouth: the sweetness of success. My son did not often experience pure joy, but there it was. His body relaxed into the accomplishment, and his smile seemed to run out of face. On the drive home, he started what has become a ritual negotiation over the restrictions we had set for a driver's license: a 7:00 P.M. curfew with the car, limiting trips to a ten-mile radius of the house, and no interstate driving. His license was ten minutes old, and the restrictions were already a burden. "Don't push it," I warned, and for once he didn't seem to care about having the last word.

He returned at 6:59 P.M. that first night of driving alone. Busy with dinner and the news, I called from the kitchen, "How was it?"

"How was what?" he asked drifting through, stopping to grab a handful of grated cheese and stuff it into his mouth. "How was the driving?" I prodded, forgetting to ask him to pick up the cheese he had dropped on the floor.

"Oh, that. That was great."

CHAPTER THIRTY-TWO

GRADUATION TO NOWHERE

I began planning Jack's high school graduation when he was four years old. Envisioning centerpieces for the far-off graduation was an antidote to the weeks of testing and evaluation that had become a routine part of my life with our son. Child developmental prognosticators warned me that he might not achieve the success. Never mind. Here's the plan. On Graduation Day friends and family will gather in the backyard for supper. As soon as possible, the graduates will wander off for a night of revelry, as tradition demands. Adults will be left to wonder how our children will ever make it through the next four years of college because each one is more clueless than the next. The following day, Sam, Jack, and I will board a flight for Caracas. The tramp steamer *M/V Amazing Grace* leaves Caracas for its 6,600-mile round trip along coastal South America. The three of us are booked to sail.

This celebratory trip has been a certainty for me since I picked up the *Tramp Steamer News* and discovered the *Amazing Grace.* I know each stateroom, each deck, and the job options for the three of us—because everyone aboard works. For the next thirteen years, I investigated hiking and helicopter rides, assembled maps and mosquito netting, and learned how to navigate by the stars.

Jack's high-school graduation is now two months away. Everything was planned. All that remains is graduation and mass assembly of the centerpieces.

This morning the school called to ask that we withdraw Jack from high school and begin his transition to adult disabilities services. He doesn't have anything close to the credits he needs for graduation, and he hasn't been in school in nearly three weeks.

A meeting called for the following day was short, considering we were ending Jack's high-school career short of graduation.

"Services and help are here for you, Jack, but you have to want to use them and you need to care about succeeding." This last line was spoken softly by one of Jack's favorite people, a counselor who had just completed a summary of appalling failure and missed opportunities that characterized Jack's high-school career.

"I don't want the help, and I don't care about success," Jack said.

"Then this meeting is over. You can't stay in school if you don't work. There is nothing more we can do for you."

"That's fine with me," Jack said. He was headed for the door. Passing very close to me on his way out of the room, he turned his face away, leaving me with the tight line of his retreating shoulders.

Opportunities for learning had been tried and trashed many times in the course of Jack's uneven path. No one was surprised. It was hope alone that propelled my belief in high-school graduation. Nothing we had seen supported my faith that he could achieve this badge of competency. But I still believed, and

I still planned. Over the years these plans and expectations became a sanctuary where I could retreat when I needed the protection of constancy.

Jack's teachers let a minute pass and realized that neither Sam nor I was going to speak. Sitting there, fully aware of what I'd heard, I still saw the party, the centerpieces, and the interior of the stateroom that would be our summer home.

Some awkward assurances that we would get together soon with the school staff were the last words I heard before heading down the hallway. Walking to the car, Sam held my hand and told me we could take the trip without the milestone of graduation. Suddenly flooded with pain, my body stopped cooperating, and the graceful exit I had planned fell apart. Pressure and heat filled my lungs, and I couldn't stop shaking. Sam pulled me to his side.

"Remember how we do it. Take one step, then another step. And remember to breathe."

He is right. That is how we do it.

C H A P T E R T H I R T Y - T H R E E

LEAVING HOME WITHOUT A KEY

Expulsion from high school didn't seem to bother Jack, and I found myself speculating on how long he had planned this failure, engineering every step with his usual disregard for the havoc created by another incendiary device dropped in the bottomless pit of failed attempts to get an education. He wasn't an annoyance, because he didn't show up in our lives, preferring the solitary confinement of his room and the late night partying with new friends I didn't like and didn't trust. Within a few weeks his decline seemed complete when a police officer called to tell us Jack had been picked up on a minor drug charge. I wasn't surprised—we knew he was using. What surprised me was my disappointment that jail time wasn't part of the deal. I planned to use the time to clean his room and find the rest of the stash. Sam hired an attorney and took him to court, and I stayed away from the house for as many hours a day as I could. After a few months, his case was dismissed and his record expunged.

"So now I'm dismissed because I haven't gotten in any more trouble with the police." Jack was belligerent.

178

The fact that he had completed the waiting period for the adjournment in contemplation of dismissal seemed to him to close the book on the experience.

"Why can't you forget about it?" This was one of the questions he asked me repeatedly. Usually he also told me he didn't need an attorney, and he would have just paid the fine. That prompted me to remind him that he had no money at the time of the arrest, before he was working. In fact, getting the job was a condition of living at home after he was arrested: Get a job and get your high school equivalency (GED) or leave. Jack sat in astonished silence, listening to our "ridiculous punishment for a little weed."

During the weeks after his arrest, the need to have him out of our life became an obsession. Like a deflated helium zephyr, I fell to the ground and couldn't get up. Hiding in bed and then inside the confines of my house didn't provide any answers. I wanted Jack to go. It wasn't just the arrest and his "no big deal" attitude about getting caught with weed. I thought I understood that part. Teenagers have little respect for the laws that govern marijuana and delight in making a benign comparison between alcohol (something Jack does not use) and the scotch and wine consumed by their hypocritical parents who frown on drugs. We were exhausted with reminding him that we were adults and whatever the evils of alcohol, it was not illegal, and we used it responsibly. I was wasting my breath.

Recently we had engaged in a nasty tug of war with the school district. They were tired of Jack's lack of resolve, although he was entitled to services until his twenty-first birthday. I believed the school had wished us out of their scope of responsibility the day he was asked to leave high school. Normally reticent friends urged Jack's immediate departure from our home, and we couldn't have agreed more. However, it turned out it is not so easy to force your child out of your home unless he commits a crime or becomes severely mentally ill.

Even if Jack was to meet the criteria of these highly undesirable circumstances, the best we could expect was a respite of a few weeks (barring a serious crime that involved jail time). Older teenagers are not attractive to the mental health system, and there are few residential options other than private-pay stints in a rehabilitation facility that can cost up to $6,000 a week. Emergency psychiatric care buys around seventy-two hours, a prescription for antidepressants, and a recommendation for individual and family therapy. This would be nothing new.

Jack, unlike many of his acting-out friends, had not already been expelled from his home. Other mothers had shared their stories about locking out their sons. I learned when boys who are not emotionally disturbed are forced to leave by parents weary of the flagrant abuse of rules or dangerous behavior that puts the family at risk, they migrate to the house of a friend where they are welcomed for a day or two at the most. These kids had homes to return to, but they didn't want restrictions placed on their freedom. In turn, their parents were tired of teenage drinking and drug use and worried about unprotected sex. Except for the rare boy, all of these kids were in school, had jobs, or were doing something with their lives. Other moms told me that if their sons returned home after being asked to leave, life was altered without improving. The root problem resulting in expulsion was not solved. Any eighteen-year-old convinced they can make it on the street, no matter how unrealistic that claim, confronts rules and restrictions with a new surliness. "Just kick me out" becomes a chant in response to demands for responsible or civil behavior. One mom said, "Trust was broken the day I told him to go. I don't think we'll ever have any sort of relationship again."

When we reached the point where Jack slept all day, left for hours with no indication of where he was going, and limited his communications to brief but obscene transactions, I no longer cared if we had a future relationship. Once or twice we called the police to track his whereabouts, taking them up on their offer to find out where he was. He always came home at night, long after we were in bed.

We didn't kick him out then. The truth was, we feared for his life on the streets. Once shunned, we believed, he would never return. Some days this vision seemed desirable, even healthy. As we assessed our options to force Jack out of our home, I was visited again by my old nemesis—uncertainty about what the hell was wrong with our son. Always denied clarity about the dysfunction we thought was some form of emotional disability, I had also been denied some internal radar that would guide us to tailored solutions especially fitted to Jack's intolerance for life's challenges.

Beyond the practical problems of showing Jack the door, there were other consequences to be considered. Teenagers who asked to leave their homes usually return when the money runs out and the friend's house is no longer hospitable. You either let them in or call the police. You get a restraining order and when the police come, you can have your child arrested. Was this to be our new family life? A round of court appearances, calls to the police, and arrests seemed a feeble ending to the distance we had traveled together as a family.

With no good alternative, we waited and watched for hopeful signs from Jack. After several weeks, he got a part-time job and managed to get himself to GED tutoring once a week.

Some weeks his paycheck actually spanned seven days of expenses, postponing the eternal arguments about his money and how he spent it. The three of us were coasting without a map and I knew it. While there was no reason to hope for change, there wasn't much drama either. I had learned to expect very little from Jack. That's exactly what I got.

CHAPTER THIRTY-FOUR

WE WILL ALWAYS HAVE BALTIMORE

An uneasy peace settled around Jack and me, like rust on an old car. But I didn't want to stress the engine that drove our tenuous union. So I was surprised that I invited Jack to Baltimore and even more surprised that he accepted.

We did have a history of mother-son trips. After some travel disasters, we had managed some successful trips together, usually just the two of us. I'd spread out a map and use a protractor to navigate a 250-mile circle with home as its center. Putting Jack's finger on the circle he'd close his eyes, peek, and move his hand until it stopped. That was our destination. We'd hop in the car, taking only what we were wearing, spending no more than $100 for essentials along the way. Activities were planned on a park bench where we would sit until someone spoke to us. Once acquainted, we'd ask our new friend about our destination, seeking advice about wonderful things to do. This led us to a blindfolded bowling tournament, a pie-eating contest where Jack finished a respectable fifth place, and a race through cherry Jell-O that will always be my personal favorite.

183

By nightfall, we'd find a hotel, order in pizza, and watch cartoons or movies until I fell asleep. It was paradise.

We had hit Baltimore once or twice when Jack's finger purposefully veered off course, leaving us both laughing. Similar straying outside the circle put us on an all-night train to Washington, DC, for a visit to the Vietnam Wall at 2:00 A.M. Jack helped me track down and trace the names of five friends and a cousin lost in that conflict, wondering at my tears so many years removed from my loss.

This latest mother-son trip to Baltimore would be made in recognition of our détente. He had dropped tutoring, worked full time, and stayed out of trouble with the police.

"If you could have had another son, you would have." The jet was taxiing for a takeoff and the question came out of nowhere. I thought carefully before answering.

"Sometimes I wonder what it would be like if it hadn't been so hard. I didn't know how to help you. I blamed myself, thought I wasn't good enough, that I wasn't the right mom for you." It was too late for feel-good stories. He was a young man. I owed him that much for broaching this conversation.

His eyes held onto mine. Jack was beautiful. I knew I had to start saying handsome. But I would always think "beautiful" until I corrected myself. I wanted a freeze frame, a minute to compose my thoughts. As many mothers know, everything important happens in the car or when you have a migraine and your significant other is someplace else. This was just a variation on the theme, the two of us on the last flight of the day to Baltimore.

"What do you want me to say?"

"I want to know if you wanted to give me back. Just a few weeks ago you wanted me to leave. No offense, Mom, but you seem to want to get rid of me pretty often." His eyes never left me, as though he was waiting for the dodge, the put-off.

He was right. After all the trial and error, we ultimately went for the dump when we couldn't push ourselves through another day. I started to talk a couple of times, and fearful of tears, stopped. His attention seemed to wander. I started to speak as the steward brought my Coke.

"You are my son. Nothing will change that. Families struggle, but we have had more to deal with than other families. Actually, that's crap. Everybody has stuff. I really don't know why it is so hard, Jack. All I know is we have had a hard time loving each other." I stopped talking.

"It's me; you and Dad were fine without me."

"You need to help me here because I want to tell you what you need to know." I didn't want this conversation anymore.

"Nothing. I don't need you to say anything. It's just, you seem like you don't care as much about what happens to us, to Dad and me. You don't yell anymore. You don't call me ten times a day."

"I thought that irritated you."

"It does. It's just that I knew where you were when you always called." He confessed this like a small child, embarrassed and defiant.

"I stopped calling when you stopped talking to me. All you said was, 'I can't talk now.' When I thought you were making terrible choices, I yelled. It's not a bad thing to want everything to be perfect for your child. It just isn't real. Nobody gets that."

"Yeah, prepare the child for the path, not the path for the child." He quoted one of the signs that hang over my desk to remind me that I can't fix the world so Jack can function within

185

it. Jack hates the encouraging "wish upon a star" sayings strewn around my work space.

"That's actually true, but that's not there to help you. That's there for me. Something that would help you would sound different." What did I have to say that would help him? I had no inspiration from all the words that fill a writer's day. But language tumbled out of my mouth anyway and landed between us.

"I hope that you love yourself as much as I love you, but I hope it means more. I do care what happens to you. I can't be in this much pain. Being your mother is like chasing the wind: great highs, then devastating lows. I made a lot of mistakes. I wanted you to be whole, free of the baggage of your disabilities. I won't lie about that—you must know that I wanted your life to be easier."

Jack was quiet, looking out the airplane's tiny window.

"I'm all right. Things were never that bad—just school and people at me all the time. You were at me a lot. I like my life; I know it's not how you thought it would be. I mean, Dad's a lawyer and you do whatever you do—important stuff. People know who you are. Nobody knows my friends' parents. They're not in the newspaper and on the radio and stuff. Unless they get arrested, then someone might hear about them."

Overcome by a desire to hold Jack in my lap, I had to back off into my corner of the cramped airline seat. I would never do that again.

He stopped to gauge my reaction.

"It's a joke, Mom."

"I know it is. It's pretty funny." We don't share any DNA, but my smart-ass gene found a way to be dominant.

On our day in Baltimore, we made a trip to the über sports center video game paradise known as the ESPN Zone in

Baltimore's Inner Harbor. The temperature in the crowded hallway registered on my body's broken thermometer at just shy of incineration. It was St. Patrick's Day, and I was neither Irish nor drunk, two conditions that might have mitigated my growing irritation.

Jack was lost to me in the crowd. The parade of patrons was pushed rather than led through the dining room to promised seating. Cresting the river of noise, I felt rather than saw the direction change. Couples in front of the line began the chicken dance in time to James Brown's rendition of "Twist and Shout," blistering through the sound system with enough force to perforate the cortex of my right brain.

High over the crowd, two long arms that I recognized as Jack's. He gestured wildly, certain I had not spotted him. Six other people did see him and changed course, following him to a sunken pit full of recliner chairs arranged theater style. At my arrival he explained to the confused seat-seekers that he wasn't a waiter and the chairs were for us, including me in the sweep of his arm.

"Wow!" Jack was upbeat and in the moment. Directly in front of our assigned recliners were forty-foot screens, each one featuring a different sport. "Look, extreme off-road racing," Jack shouted over the cacophony of deafening bass. "This summer Mike and I are going to Florida to this track, this same track right here on the screen. I can't wait to crank up one of those babies.

"Can you believe this place? Thanks, Mom. I'm having a great time. I'm glad we're here," he trailed off, taking it all in; the noise, the crowd, the perky blonde with the minimal breast coverage and the tattooed snake head slithering down her chest.

Did he just say thanks? Did my son tell me he was having fun with me? Shut up, everyone, I want that moment back. My hand reached out to the vicinity of his arm, halting only after I knocked over his drink. Jack escaped the flowing water and any intentions I might have had by bouncing to his feet to hear the waitress's question.

Eyeing her cleavage with surprising finesse (every time she made eye contact, his eyes were already on her face as though it floated above an uninteresting body), Jack spoke to her ear either to avoid shouting or improve his view. Her left breast was named "Jodi," and I assumed that covered the rest of her. She asked if he wanted a bottle or a draft.

"I'm sticking with Coke," he answered putting off the inevitable identity check.

"Great!" She was even perkier. "Finally, I have a customer who isn't drunk. I hate St. Patrick's Day. The Coke's on me."

Jodi was thrilled with his sobriety. "You're a big boy, aren't you?" Jodi smiled, raking her eyes up his six-foot-four-inch frame, while Jack gave her a grin I had never seen before. As she wrote the order, he threw me a desperate glance that pleaded, "Don't tell her how old I am (eighteen)." The only words I could have produced were, "Let's get the hell out of here."

"What can I you for you, ma'am?" Assuming she was speaking to the shriveled-up old woman on her dream date's left, I gave her an order for iced tea.

"Look, mad recliner seats." In youth speak, mad means "more than acceptable," not demented or on the edge of sanity. That would be me.

Attacking the leather recliner in a full frontal assault, Jack landed face down, flipped over his body, and pulled the lever forward, jerking up to a sitting position. I crawled self-consciously into my own seating apparatus that appeared to be a loveless marriage between a La-Z-Boy and a waterbed. An attached tray for drinks and food completed the ensemble. Once reclined, I couldn't get any leverage, because I couldn't reach the handle. An uncoordinated skirmish to keep my head from sliding under the food tray resulted in a half-sitting position. Peeking out over the tray table, I determined that my breasts could either rest on top of the table or be pinned underneath it, perhaps making the more elegant statement.

"Mom, what's wrong with you? Just sit up, you look stupid."

The ESPN Zone has a flagrant policy of abuse toward little people. The sign on the opposite wall told me we were in the VIP section. Apparently I was allowed in, even though I didn't meet the height requirement. Deaf and physically disabled by the amenities, I quieted down and waited for Jodi's return, searching the screen for a preview of Jack's summer plans.

Top-heavy race cars crashed into concrete side walls, rolled eight or nine times, and sometimes released a parachute before coming to a halt. The smoky violence and the drivers' near-death experiences mesmerized Jack. My eyes crossed at the proximity of the death match, and a wave of dizziness threatened my precarious balance in the chair. The neighboring screen was no help: mammoth trucks powered by skyscraper-size tires vaulted over smaller trucks in a car crushing exercise I couldn't grasp.

Jodi returned with tasty food, touching Jack's neck and arm more often than was strictly necessary to deliver a cheeseburger. She called him "babe" or "hon" in her excessive trips to his chair. We're in the South, I reasoned. Well, we're south of New Jersey. Wait staff call everyone "hon." Except Jodi repeatedly called me "ma'am." Soon I had adjusted to the noise and found a certain peace in the senseless truck crossings.

A system for getting the food to my mouth from a tray three inches below my chin was working flawlessly if I kept my head at the right angle. I didn't hear Jack's voice seeping through the surround sound.

"What do you think, Mom?" My guess was that his question had been repeated more than once, and Jack's face confirmed my suspicion that he had been speaking while I was shoveling a veggie wrap.

"What do I think about what?" I was forced to ask. I sat up extra straight to make up for my lapse.

"What about getting my GED? Maybe you could hire the tutor again. I could try it."

I was not cool. I did not causally say, "Sure, let's give it a try." I let him wait there, unable to still the fear of squandering this opportunity because it happened while sitting in the ESPN Zone in Baltimore on St. Patrick's Day.

"Well, ah, I, ah, I...think that's a good plan," I finished pitifully.

Apparently he wasn't finished with the conversation we had begun on the airplane flying south. I had no idea where he was going, but he was talking. Fighting my affinity for filling the awkward gaps, I bit my lip. After a break for an especially graphic off-road disaster, his attention was fully on my face. He looked nervous.

"If I lived with another family, I would have been kicked out by now. Maybe the dad would have beaten me up or even killed me. Why do you let me stay? Don't tell me because you love me." Jack was adamant.

"Okay, I don't love you." I barely got out the words. I wanted to him to believe in the solidarity of the family we had built in spite of the odds against it. I didn't bother to hide my distress, and for a moment he seemed to realize he'd gone too far.

"No, Mom, I know you love me, but that's not why you let me stay," he answered me.

"What makes you so sure?" I asked.

"I heard you that night, after I got arrested for possession. You were crying a lot, and you told Dad that I broke your heart. You said you couldn't stay around to watch me destroy my life. You said you wondered if my birth mother wanted me back." He didn't accuse me. He just said it all as though he was telling me I had mustard on my face.

"I did say those things. I'm sorry that you heard me."

"I knew you were really mad, because you didn't talk to me for a week. You didn't come to court with me either. You must have been really spazzed out."

"You do not know what it is like to have your child arrested, Jack. I know you thought the marijuana charge was no big deal. That's the way things are today; drug arrests for marijuana are no big deal. To me, it was a big deal."

"That is so stereotypical." Jack used his favorite word to describe my old-world ways and my 1960's thinking. Those liberating and restless years had shaped my life and values, even defined my ideals of parenting: I would be open, accepting, and respectful of my child's privacy. It was all good until I actually had a child and was forced to view the world from the perspective of his safety, not my adolescent fantasy. Jack wasn't interested in my experiences. He had the *History Channel* and *YouTube*, and he knew it all. I was too old and completely unconnected to his world.

When he asked me if I'd ever used pot, I told him the truth.

"Yes, I did. For maybe six months."

"Then why do you keep telling me it's bad for me?"

"Because smoking weed is bad for you. Pot is more potent than what we got at eighteen. Our state has Neanderthal drug laws. If you're using, you're buying. Dealers are not your friends. There are so many things that can go wrong. You could go to jail."

I usually couldn't help myself and often capped off my comments with the thing that mattered least to him: "Your dad is an attorney. People need to trust him. You get busted again, and it will get in the paper. That will be embarrassing and will make Dad seem ridiculous to his clients and colleagues."

This response invariably resulted in throwing under the bus the other kids he knew who were regular users and who had an attorney parent.

God, I felt like a hypocrite. The whole argument made me tired and depressed, just as Jack had designed it to do. How different was I from my son at age eighteen? I had smoked marijuana. I never got arrested, and when I had to make the choice between pot and beer, it wasn't even a contest. I couldn't afford both, and I was always a little on the fringe with the potheads anyway. None of this made me a hero. My son's arrest for possession hadn't destined him for a life of crime either. Why couldn't I drop it?

But our circular argument wasn't really about pot. It was about Jack having no filter, no capacity to see beyond what his friends believed. A new friend who would gain ascendancy tomorrow could convince him to give up pot, drink shooters and beer, or join the Peace Corps. He didn't have the emotional resolve to make many of his own decisions. The only thing he knew was that I was wrong. Total strangers and second cousins of friends of friends received more respect and more loyalty than Sam or me.

And it made me furious.

A long pause filled the space that usually contained Jack's comeback argument. I looked over at him. He seemed spent, nearly as tired as I had become of solving this timeless riddle of conflicting parent-child values.

"It's your life now, Jack. I've known that for a while. Of course I want you to try as hard as I tried to make your life go. You'll do it your way. I'll love you forever and ever. When I said I wanted to send you back, it was because I couldn't watch you make bad decisions anymore, and you didn't want my help. You still have me, us, our family. That's the truth."

"I'll always love you, Mom." The relentless sounds of extreme sports quieted, moving away to the middle distance of my thoughts. Deep inside my soul, a fissure closed, healing a wound that had hurt forever.

"Then we made it, Jack. We made it. Life is probably not what either one of us wanted, but we love each other. That counts."

He didn't let go of my eyes, and his head nodded slowly. His attention shifted to the screen, and after a few minutes he turned back to me.

"So you'll hire the tutor?"

"You have to go every time, and you have to pay half."

"So much for fuzzy-love talk, I guess." He was right. His eyes lost the intensity of their focus as Jodi came into view. The noise had stopped, and most of the luncheon crowd was gone. Jack stood up to lean over Jodi, hugging her. My God, relationships move fast. What would have happened if he'd had a beer?

"Thanks for coming in." Jodi looked at me. "Are you his mom?" I liked this girl.

"Yes," I admitted.

"My mom died when I was young. It's great you two go places together."

"Yeah, my mom is mostly okay." Jack gave me a crooked smile. My cup runneth over.

They traded e-mail addresses and cell phone numbers while I paid the bill and pretended not to notice her age, her breasts, and her tattoos.

We spent the rest of the afternoon in the Baltimore Aquarium. Jack moved through an aquarium like a stingray, noticing, reacting, and rejoicing. I go along to watch him loving the water creatures and to glimpse an occasional seahorse. We fought over where to have dinner. He wanted room service, and I wanted Little Italy. He went out to eat with me without grace or patience. Jodi called three times when we got back to the hotel room. He took the calls in the bathroom and announced at 11:30 that he was going out for an hour.

"Be careful, and have fun."

He turned around and looked at me as though I had agreed to purchase an off-road vehicle and begin crashing immediately into walls.

"I can go?" He was incredulous.

"Yeah, go ahead. Be back in an hour, no more."

Ten minutes after he left, I began to pace the hotel hallway and then back and forth to the window overlooking the Inner Harbor from the nineteenth floor. Twenty minutes into his absence I checked the telephone number for the Harbor Police. He knew his way around the Inner Harbor. He had returned, alone, to this same hotel when he was twelve. He lived at boarding school for three years. I read the same page of the *Baltimore Sun* dozens of times. Jack was back in fifty-five minutes, happy and content.

"I walked Jodi to her bus when she got off of work. Her brother is my age, and she likes younger men."

The next day I was searching the sky from 29,000 feet aboard another late-night flight home. I waited for the lights of home to appear in the dark, cloudless sky. We had been away forty-eight hours, yet more than a lifetime had passed between Jack and me. My son was across the aisle, traveling solo. Pressing my face into the tight space of the Plexiglas porthole, my eyes filled with tears I hadn't cried in months. In the busy laughter of the full airplane, I could sit with my loss, welcoming this rupture, this split of his young life separating from mine.

I know something now that I never guessed until Baltimore: you don't let go of your children when you're ready. They let go of you whether you're ready or not.

A tap on my left arm warned me of a hand moving across my lap.

"Look at the stars," said the voice from the man compressed into the seat next to mine.

A brilliant constellation lit the sky next to the wing. I don't remember the constellations and hoped I wasn't in for an astronomy lesson. Instead, my sky partner turned off our overhead lights, bringing the stars into bright focus. The chain of light played around the wing for a long time, making it shine and dance. During our descent, we moved under the cloud cover, losing the nighttime sky to the heavens.

Once on the ground, Jack pulled our bags from the bins above his head. Anticipating the requests, he stood still as the old and the short realized how handy he was to have on an airplane, one by one asking for help with their luggage. He was used to providing overhead bin service and by now may think it is part of his ticket price.

Sam was as far through the gate as one is allowed in these times when everyone fears their neighbors, and the threat of terrorism is foisted upon us in yellow, orange, and red alerts. Sam looked tired and wonderful. I couldn't wait to tell him— what? That I was okay? That our son was going to be okay? That we would be okay? Sam kissed me, shook Jack's hand and helped me with my luggage. Jack's cell phone began to ring. By the third call he was asking to be dropped at home to pick up a car.

"I made corned beef for dinner," Sam offered.

"That's okay, Dad. I had *Taco Bell* at the airport. Don't you love St. Patrick's Day? Mom will eat the corned beef; she's been complaining since this afternoon. She wants corned beef."

Deposited at the garage to pick up a car, Jack leaned through the window to kiss me, thanking me for the trip.

"What was that about? Since when does he say thank you?" Sam was puzzled. "You've only been gone two days. What did you give him?"

"Love," I said. "I gave him our love."

CHAPTER THIRTY-FIVE

SAYING GOOD-BYE

The quirky, zippy boy I could not heal may find a place in the world that's all his own. Or he may struggle with the anxiety, the pressure to conform, and insufficient coping skills that have overwhelmed him, and us, for years. Whatever happens, Jack continues to be the architect of his own life, rejecting help in any form.

My son is different, often self-destructive and anxious. He didn't choose his wiring system, and I fought the truth of DNA and temperament with every weapon I could gather. Jack is also a meticulous witness, capable of differentiating the sound of a 737 and a 757 from half a mile away. He can spot a tumor on his cat's back by the way her fur ruffles. He can explain the colors in his dad's daylilies so that a sightless person might rejoice in the artistry of nature. He has my wicked sense of humor and his dad's unfailing radar for justice.

In a last-ditch effort to pull him through his GED and access community college and work, Sam and I brought a legal action to force the school, the adult vocational system, and the therapists to act together, assisting Jack in crossing a mystical finish line into adult life. Five months of expensive, time-consuming litigation enraged the school district, frustrated employment coaches and therapists, and pushed Sam and me to the brink of insanity. But we got what he needed to close the holes that most threaten Jack's future.

Exhausted but hopeful, I explained how this new structure of enhanced tutoring and job skill development would bring him the rest of the way to his dream of working with cars. He was flat out uninterested in anything we had to offer. Two minutes into my explanation, Jack cut me off, upset his chair in the zeal to leave the room, and shouted, "I don't need any help. Leave me alone. I hate that you can't leave me alone."

"You wanted this help, Jack. This was what you wanted so you could go to automotive or graphic design school. What did you think would happen?"

"I'm going to keep working and I'll go to the tutoring I'm doing now. I'm not doing anything else. Stop interfering."

He did ask for help passing the GED. Like many other things in his life, he didn't consider what that help would look like. Three months of unenthusiastic assistance finally came from the school and disability professionals who felt Jack had tapped all of the time, energy, and money that would be tolerated for a single child left behind. When it came time to take the exam, Jack was more prepared than I would have thought possible and seemed confident about the step he was taking. Yet on the morning of the test he got up and announced he wasn't going to the GED exam.

"I can't do it, Mom," he said without further explanation. I didn't need more information. He couldn't do it. Anxiety fluttered in through the windows and took away his fragile courage and resolve. But, three weeks later he went to the test, finished early, and passed on the first try. Last year he applied to and was accepted by a local community college where his major changes twice a semester. He even passes some classes and the teachers tell me they love his humor and intellectual curiosity. Who knew?

I believe I have learned to let his life develop without the intervention of my personal guidance system. I may even loosen my grip on the throat of the world that will not welcome Jack until he finds the value in compromise and basic rules that ask all of us to wait in line from time to time.

In the end, I did the best I could. During Jack's childhood, I repeated this simple phrase hundreds of times and never understood the miracle scooped up and held together by those words. We are a family, tied together by happenstance, history, and love. Tested by his disabilities, I may have come up short when measured by a cosmic ruler sizing up the limits of unconditional love. Loving my child has meant sacrifice beyond any rational expectation. It was providential that Jack came to us as a baby. His innocence and his total dependency on my nascent skills at motherhood gave us both a fighting chance to bridge the havoc that would come to define our lives.

Sam and I have stayed married, continued to love each other and to love Jack. We fought depression, isolation, and each other. I hope Jack remembers that his dad and I are here, still loving him, if not helping him. I hope he'll let us in before he falters into fear and the dangerous decisions he sometimes makes. I hope, but I can't ask it anymore. He is mostly on his own, and that's the way he wants it.

I have forgiven myself for any transgressions and failures, real or imagined, although most of my self-loathing was a product of fatigue and regret. I have a son who is different, who doesn't measure up to the community standard for active, healthy children. Ironically, he doesn't measure up to the standards for disability either. He is smart, funny, capable, and missing a piece of sanity, or clarity, or who knows what?

"I appreciate what you're doing, Mom," Jack told me recently on his way out the door. He was going to miss his grandmother's eighty-fifth birthday party. The reason didn't matter. None would have satisfied me.

"What?"

"You're mad, but you're not yelling. I don't want to go to the party."

"Okay." I was moving quickly, getting together the gift and card. He watched me with quiet eyes, unworried by my disappointment.

"Tell Grandma I love her."

"Don't you think you should tell her yourself?"

"You are the best at telling people about love, Mom. You're the best."

I looked up at him, wondering just how much I was being played. He smiled, transforming that beautiful face I had known through its worst tantrums and tears. Kissing my cheek with care, my son held on to my shoulder for an extra heartbeat as we moved through the door into the pool of light dropped by the setting sun.

"I think your heart is two sizes too big," Jack said borrowing from one of his favorite Dr. Seuss stories. "I like that about you."

With this farewell, Jack made his break. Jumping through the open door of his truck, he started the engine and pulled away from the front door at a speed that usually annoyed me. I waited until his taillights faded, merging into the traffic on the highway before I told him, "I love you, too, Jack. I love you, too."

CHAPTER THIRTY-SIX

SUMMING UP

More than twenty years ago I sat in a hospital room holding Jack's birth mother in my arms. When she surrendered her baby to us, the family I'd spent years trying to shape was finally complete. Bonds of gratitude and wonder held me to her side, even as my husband guided me to the door, and whispered, "We've said our last good-byes. It's time to go." Our journey to becoming a family would be wondrous and excruciating. In that moment, each footstep was hiding in expectations I could not have seen, and in a future I would never have predicted.

I have kept my promise to love Jack forever and ever in the only way I know how: by remembering her gift and celebrating my joy at becoming a mother. Somehow, our family has survived the constant bumping between our hopes and Jack's inflexible and perplexing neurological guidance system. My memories of his childhood are different from the ones I had imagined I would treasure as a mom. I have listened to the sentiments of other mothers who have watched as their sons turned into men. I wanted to order it up, just what they had.

Accomplishment, recognition, problems solved in a blaze of family bonding. I wanted a good marriage or loving partner for him, and grandchildren for me to love with new abandon.

My eyes have been trained to look in other corners to see the shadows of our joined hearts.

The night I rocked Jack until dawn is still with me, as is the soft, spicy smell of his newborn head. I can see him at T-ball practice, something he agreed to do only once, if his grandfather came to watch him. Hearing him negotiate for a private room at the school for troubled adolescents is among my hopeful pictures. It contains the potential of his tenacious mind.

With a timepiece set to his own internal clock, Jack now manages the possibilities of his strengths. He is outdistancing the ghosts of teachers and mental health professionals who set the bar too low for him. It is slow work, but he has achieved a mighty miracle in his adaptation to emerging adulthood.

More than once, we believed we'd lost Jack—to his dysfunction or to our pain; it didn't matter. On the darkest days of his growing up I couldn't see making it to the next day, much less a future for our son. The power of his impulsivity combined with pure doggedness is imprinted in his unique wiring system. He holds the key, and until he understands his own power, I suspect that his life events will scare and concern me.

Today our son is a young man. He is funny, empathic, and generous when not pushed to perform or sustain a difficult path of discipline or resolve. He has friends who love him and who receive his loyalty and protection in return. He has the love of a beautiful young woman. Impetuous, intolerant, and troubled by a world that will not bend to his bidding, his life is surprisingly simple. It's what he wants. He went through hell to get there and pulled Sam and me along for the bumpy ride.

Years ago, for a few weeks after Jack dropped out of high school we didn't know where he lived. Reports from his friends placed him around the neighborhood. Occasionally I saw him, and sometimes he'd stop and talk to me. Once we passed each other on the road, and Jack signaled me to stop in the wide shoulder. Getting out of his car he loped towards me, hugging me through my open window. I stayed in the car for the protection I believed that I still needed.

"Hey, Mom, I wondered where you were. I miss you."

"Yes?" I asked cautiously.

"Let's have lunch sometime."

"I'd like that. Call me." His ringing phone distracted him, and he headed back to his car with it cupped to his ear. I had to pull away from the shoulder before I invited him home in exchange for that hug and a kiss. This was not a trend, this loving moment. It was only a brief glimpse into his capable heart.

We worked our way through that separation and came to a place that mimics acceptance most days. Pain, anger, guilt, and remorse were stones in the road to making peace with the person we loved the most. Eventually, we found our way back to each other and welcomed him into our home again. We still labor hour by hour at maintaining an uneasy, unsettled peace.

Jack started community college a full three years behind his graduating class. In a strange role reversal, we now hear about careers and maximum starting salaries instead of the minimum wage he was once happy to have. Any salary kept his car running for brief periods, and moved him beyond our control. Recently, he bought a well-used luxury car and is piecing together dreams. Jack rarely shares his fantasies with us, lest we find fault, or worse, praise his efforts. Jack keeps us shielded from what may be brewing as he negotiates the untried territory of routine life. We are proud of him.

Life is still messy. The sharp edges of chaos that punctured my sanctuary for so long often take me by surprise, pulling me back into the those feelings of sadness and hopelessness. I don't know how Jack will succeed in community college. He has never finished a single year of formal education. With just a scoop of plausible evidence, I am seduced by his confidence, because he would like me to trust him. I have formally withdrawn my bid to direct Jack's life. He insists on the starring role with a calm determination that astonishes me. I want exclusive rights to the part of Mom, if it is still available throughout the years.

I know that the time for making childhood memories is over. But I still remember laughter. I remember all the people who believed in us, urging us to make it through another day. Remarkable friends continued to loved us, welcoming the hurricane that was our family into the calmer waters of their own lives. There were acts of grace that broke my heart. Moms who offered endless cups of coffee and talked politics with me, pulling me back into the world I'd left behind. Once, devastated over a prognosis made during a grade-school conference that sentenced Jack to a suicide watch during school hours, my friend speculated whether my son was capable of taking his own life.

"I think he's too disorganized," I said. "By the time he gets to the kitchen for the knife, he'll forget what he's doing and ask for a peanut butter and jelly on white."

We laughed because there was no other way to shut out the horror that lurked on the other side of the door. I was safe in my kitchen. Jack was playing nearby, happy in his isolation from the everyday demands of school and life.

Finally, when he was free of childhood, he crept out on his own and began to enjoy rare and satisfying success. Whatever Jack learned from those calamitous years of childhood and school, he extracted it all on his own. He was always curious, fascinated by the world. But he was not a learner. Instead, Jack randomly absorbed what he cared about and ignored almost everything else. Right after he dropped out of high school, I asked Jack what he wanted to do. What was he willing to work for? He took a long moment before he said, "I just want to get what everyone has. I want a chance, and I'd like you and Dad to respect me. I know that's important, but I don't know how to get respect." My response to this profound understanding of all he that lacked was so simple that I'm still not sure whether or not he heard me. "Just trust yourself Jack. And tell the truth. Respect will show up." That's all I had for him because I believe that's how life works.

As I sit writing this, Jack sticks his head in my office door. "I went to the wrong class this morning." He is laughing, so I know he is managing this ubiquitous freshman nightmare.

"What are you going to do?" My voice is even, my eyes on the computer screen.

"Not a problem. I'll make it up." He moves over my chair for a kiss aimed at my forehead. Changing his focus to the screen, he misses, saying, "I can't believe you are still writing that book. Am I in the nursing home yet?"

"No, you're in college."

"Like right now, like today, in college?"

"Uh-huh, like that."

"You're never going to finish that thing if you keep following me around." He smiles into my face. Seeing something I can't translate, he laughs. This is a hopeful sound that I'm happy to witness, although I'm still fearful of my growing dependence on his better humor. I watch as his long form slips through my door and takes the steps three at a time.

He is yelling at me from near the front door. "I love you, Mom. I need boxer shorts. Get the soft ones. I hate the scratchy ones."

"OK, I'll see what I can do."

"Oh, and the cat threw up down here. Could you get it? I'm late."

Parents travel a long road with their children. Ours seems truncated, shortened by tight spirals of grief and uncertainty. We don't seem to have covered much distance for all the time we have traveled from infancy to young adult. The hairpin turns of mood swings and meltdowns make it hard to remember any stretches of contentment or family memories worth noting. But, I think making a family life together is like stitching a quilt, searching for the colors and the design that in time will become a whole, pleasing blanket. For all the missed stitches, the jarring colors, and the times we lost sight of the design altogether, we created a place to wait for the future together, and to be warm. It is enough.

ABOUT THE AUTHOR

DONNA MILLER

Donna Miller is a passionate storyteller, published writer, teacher, political analyst, speechwriter, and child advocate. Ms. Miller contributes to national and international journals on wide-ranging topics such as family relationships, child advocacy, illness, injury prevention, and travel. Donna mentors entrepreneurial activists, helping to craft social and corporate messaging that bring new ideas to life. She leads consumers to better health decision-making, and ignites support for various parenting organizations. Her work has stirred community action and kick-started cultural change. Donna Miller assists young people pursuing memoir and other arts through the establishment of the Christopher Miller Creative Arts Foundation in Troy, New York. Her second non-fiction book, *Stalking Grace* will be completed in 2015.

CPSIA information can be obtained at www.ICGtesting.com
Printed in the USA
BVOW03s2022050914

365718BV00002B/9/P